AF598735

Martha's VINEYARD

Martha's VINEYARD

PHOTOGRAPHS BY MICHAEL KAHN

TEXT BY MICHAEL KAHN AND CHRISTINE YURICK

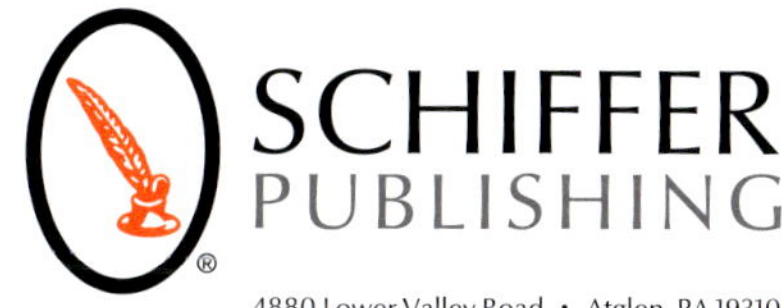

4880 Lower Valley Road • Atglen, PA 19310

Other Schiffer Books by Michael Kahn:

East Coast Atlantic Beaches, 978-0-7643-5931-6
Sailboats, 978-0-7643-5930-9
Healing Power of Water, 978-0-7643-6265-1

Library of Congress Control Number: 2020952561

Designed by Ashley Millhouse
Type set in Montserrat
Creative design and input by Christine Yurick

ISBN: 978-0-7643-6269-9
Printed in China

Published by Schiffer Publishing, Ltd.
4880 Lower Valley Road
Atglen, PA 19310
Phone: (610) 593-1777; Fax: (610) 593-2002
E-mail: Info@schifferbooks.com
Web: www.schifferbooks.com

To my editor and wife, Christine Yurick, without whom this book, and a lot of other things, would never have happened.

LITERARY CONTENTS

INTRODUCTION

When I first visited Martha's Vineyard in 1998, I was an aspiring fine-art, black-and-white-film photographer. I came to the island with a new portfolio of sailing photographs of wooden boats. I was in search of an art gallery to represent my work when Nancy Winch of the Gardner Colby Gallery in Edgartown decided to take me on. I became a fast friend with Nancy and her gallery team of Pamela and Jonathan and am still friends with them today. The island community and its visitors quickly embraced my artwork, and the island became my second home. It did not take long to realize that the island had a rich community of artistic, friendly, and welcoming people who truly cared about the beauty of the island on which they lived. I also have a strong commitment to the preservation of its natural resources, and to this day I support the local conservation organizations—the Trustees of Reservations, Sheriffs Meadow Foundation, and the Audubon Society, to name a few.

My transition to photographing seascapes was seamless because of the island's geographic diversity and incredible natural beauty. I was, and still am, an avid fisherman, and Martha's Vineyard was on my bucket list. Living out of my Volkswagen van filled with fishing rods and cameras, I spent weeks on end exploring the beaches, ponds, creeks, and jetties. Discovering and photographing this constantly changing place consumed me. Looking back, I am not sure when I slept. I always had a camera or fishing rod, or both, in my hands as I chased the sun around the island.

This book is the culmination of the past twenty-two years of hard work and great joy. Creating these photographs was truly a pleasure. I am happy to say that I still shoot film and that my work is still being represented on the island by the wonderful group of people at North Water Gallery in Edgartown. I would like to offer special thanks to my gallery, and to the residents and visitors of this little gem of an island. Here, they have managed to find a balance among community spirit, preservation, and economics. I hope you enjoy this book of photographs, and please do what you can to help preserve these fragile and important places.

ANNIVERSARY ON THE ISLAND

W. S. MERWIN

The long waves glide in through the afternoon
while we watch from the island
from the cool shadow under the trees where the long ridge
a fold in the skirt of the mountain
runs down to the end of the headland

day after day we wake to the island
the light rises through the drops on the leaves
and we remember like birds where we are
night after night we touch the dark island
that once we set out for

and lie still at last with the island in our arms
hearing the leaves and the breathing shore
there are no years anymore
only the one mountain
and on all sides the sea that brought us

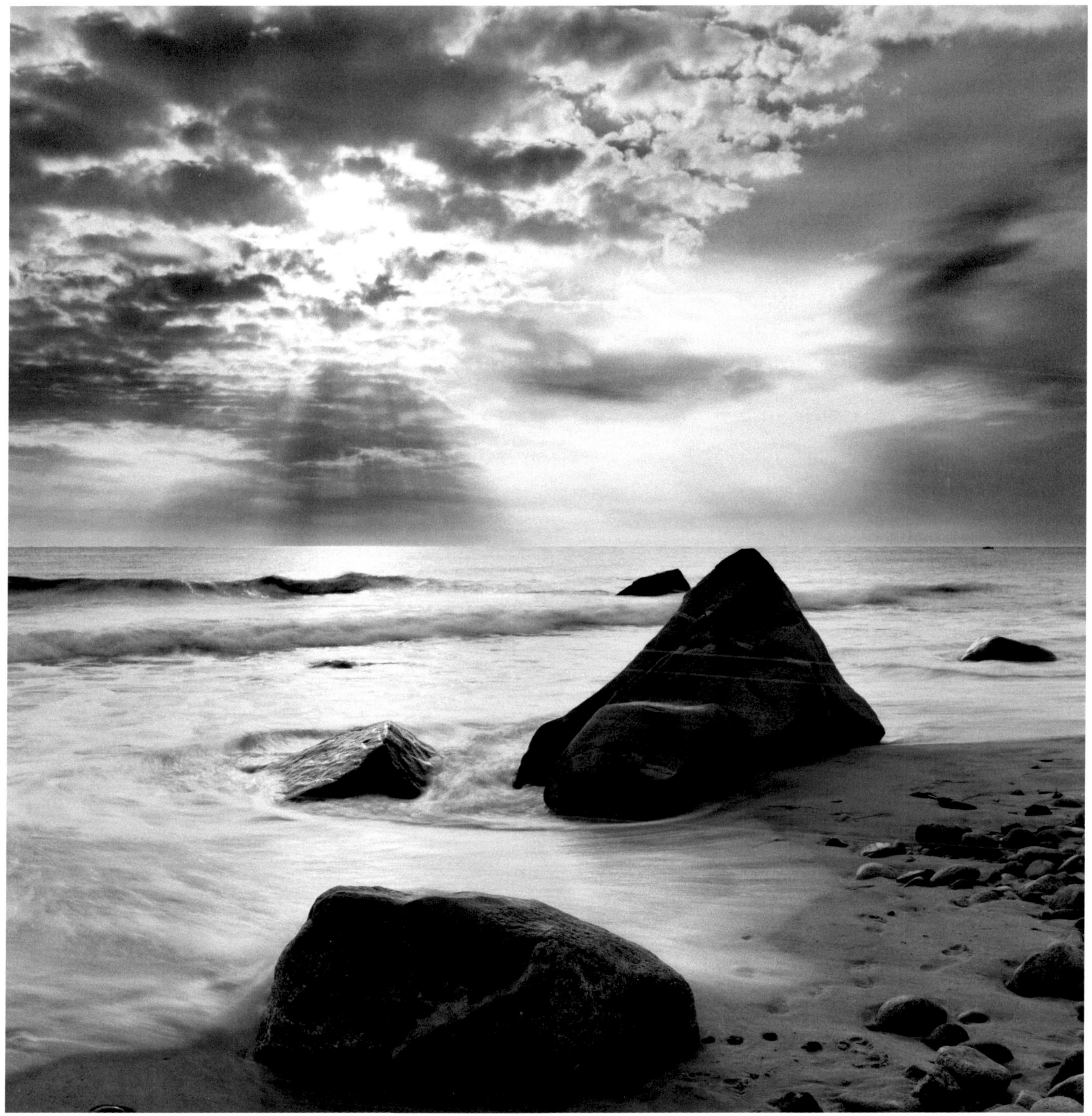

Aquinnah, 1998

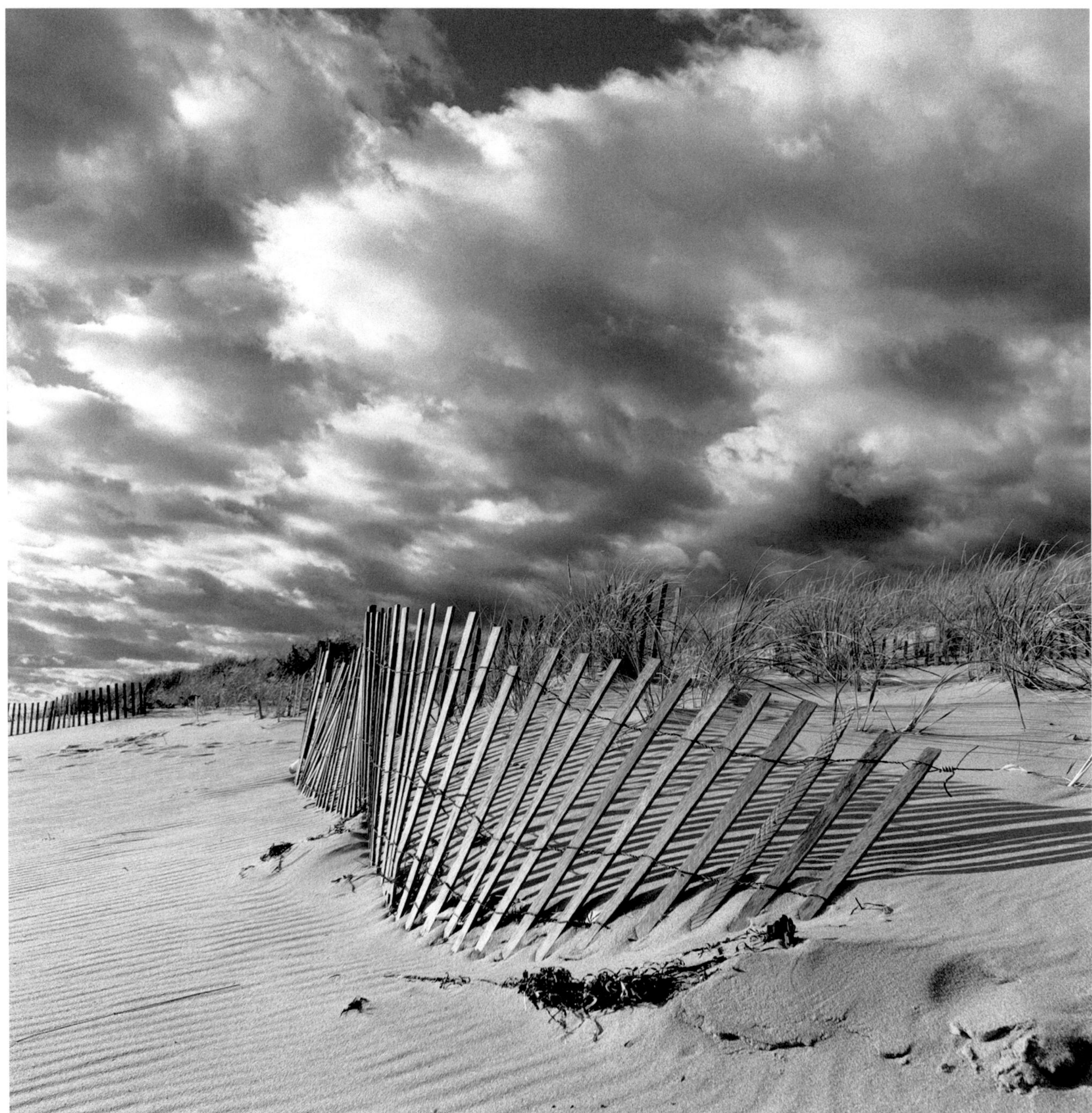

South Beach, 2006

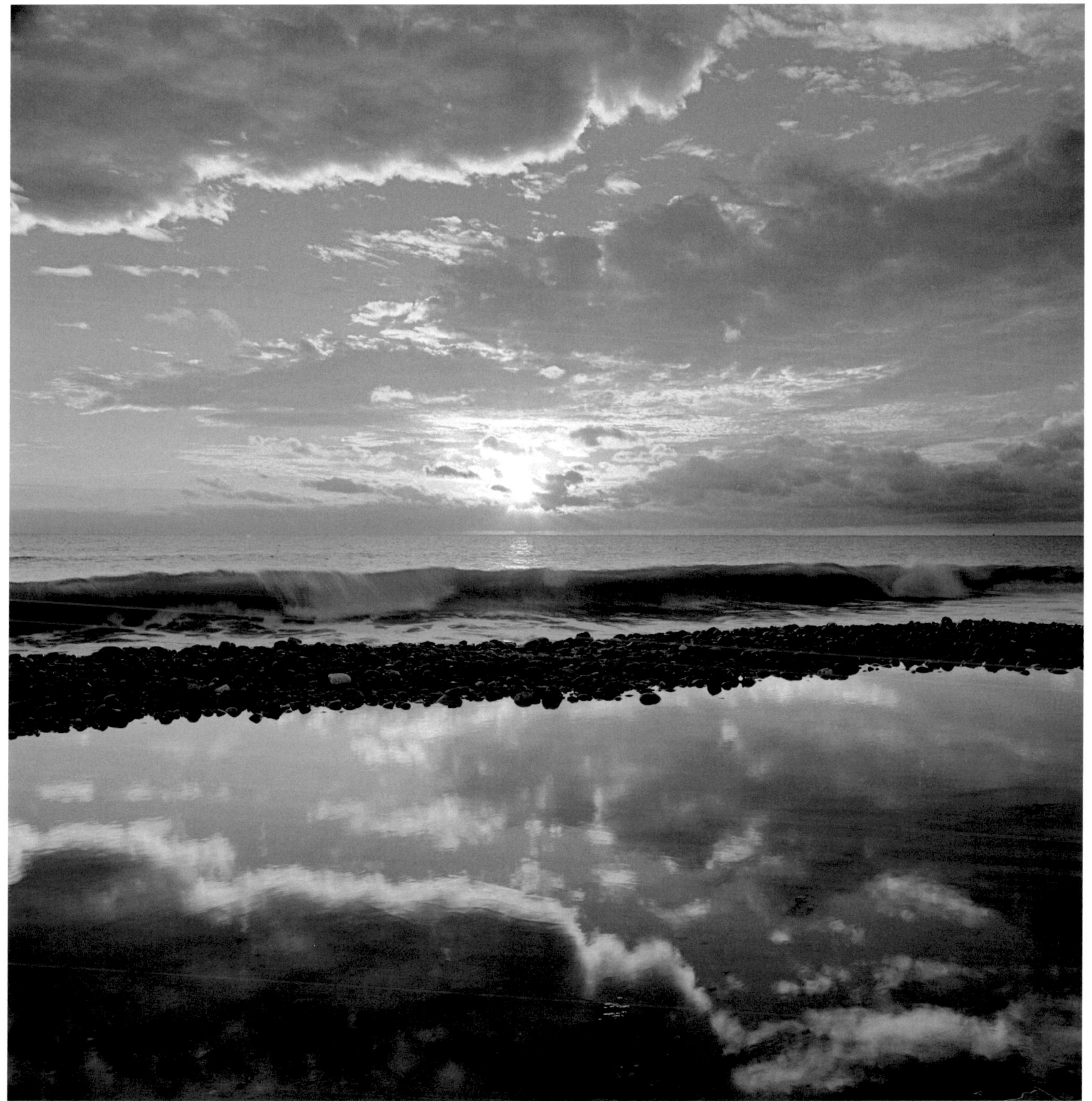

Philbin Beach, 1999

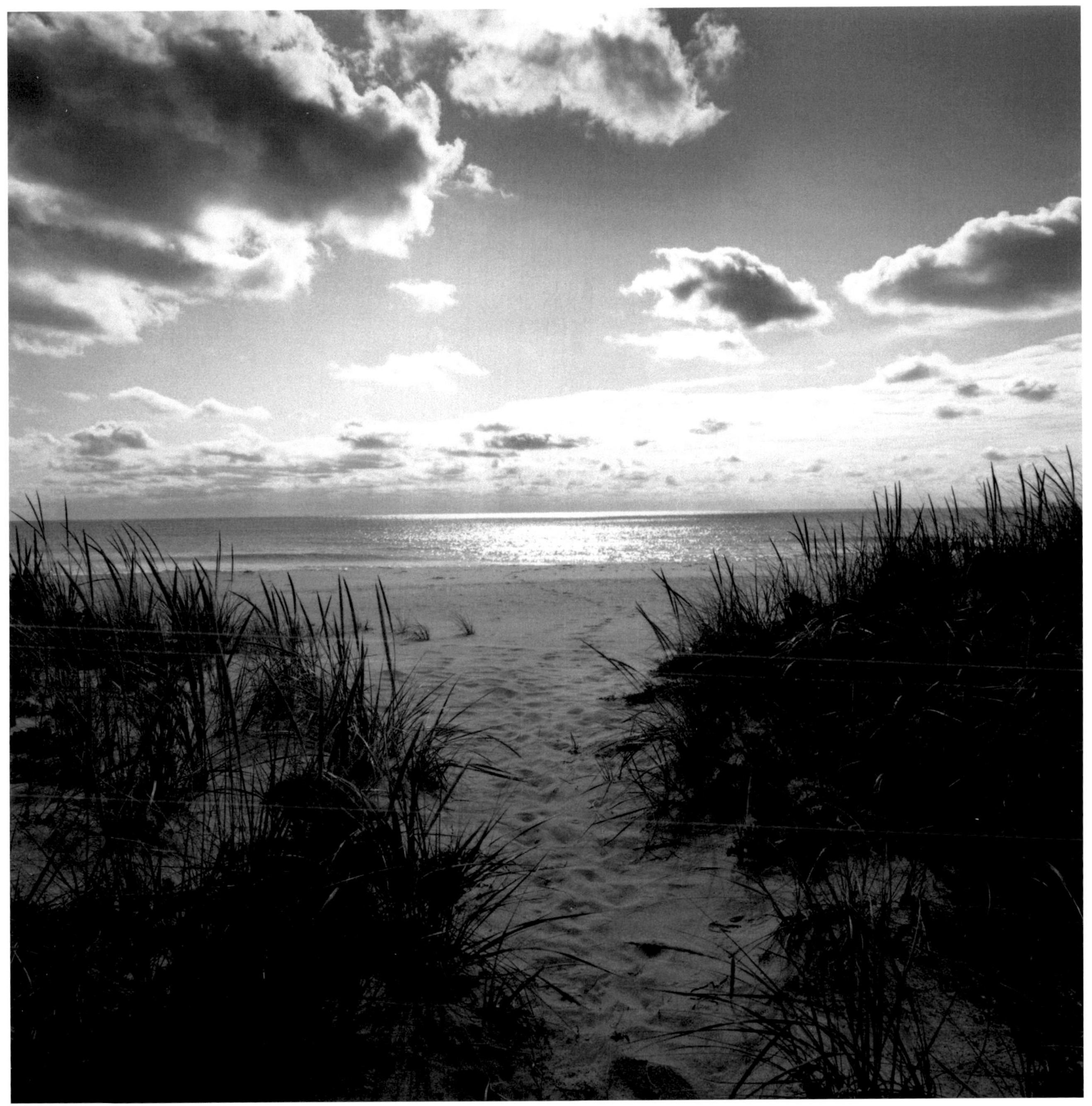

South Shore, 2006

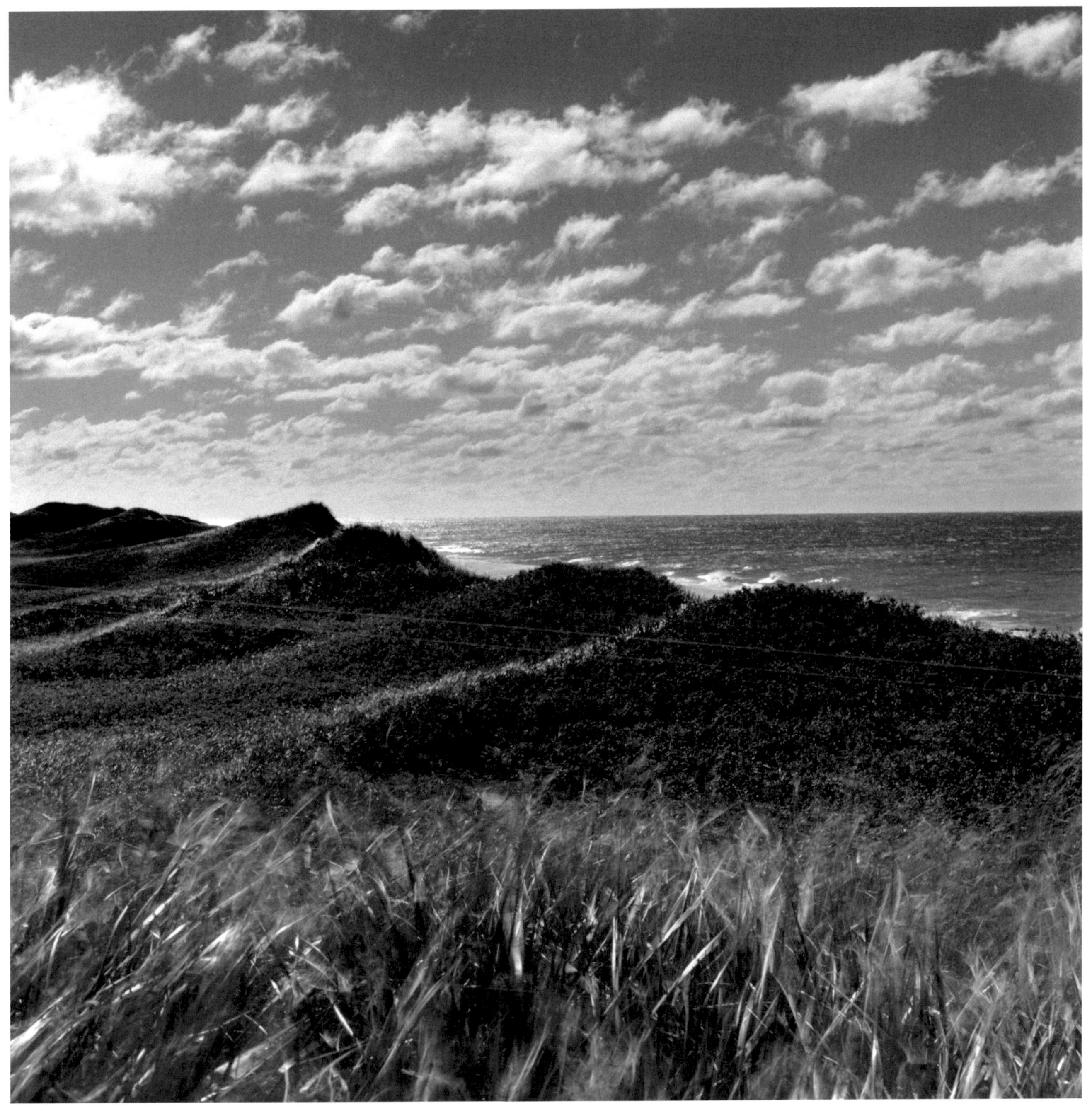

Zack's Cliffs, 2016

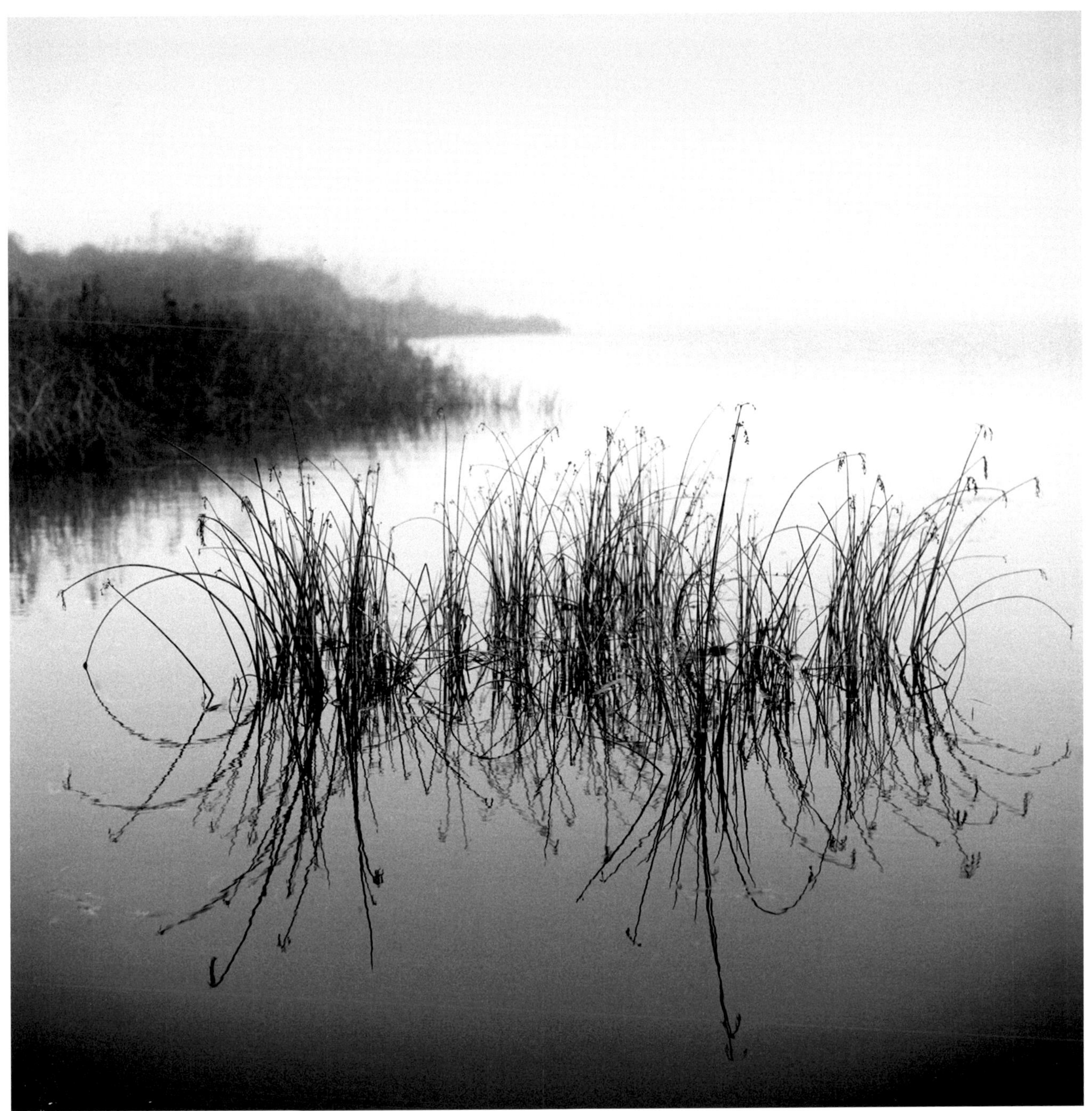

Chilmark Pond, 2004

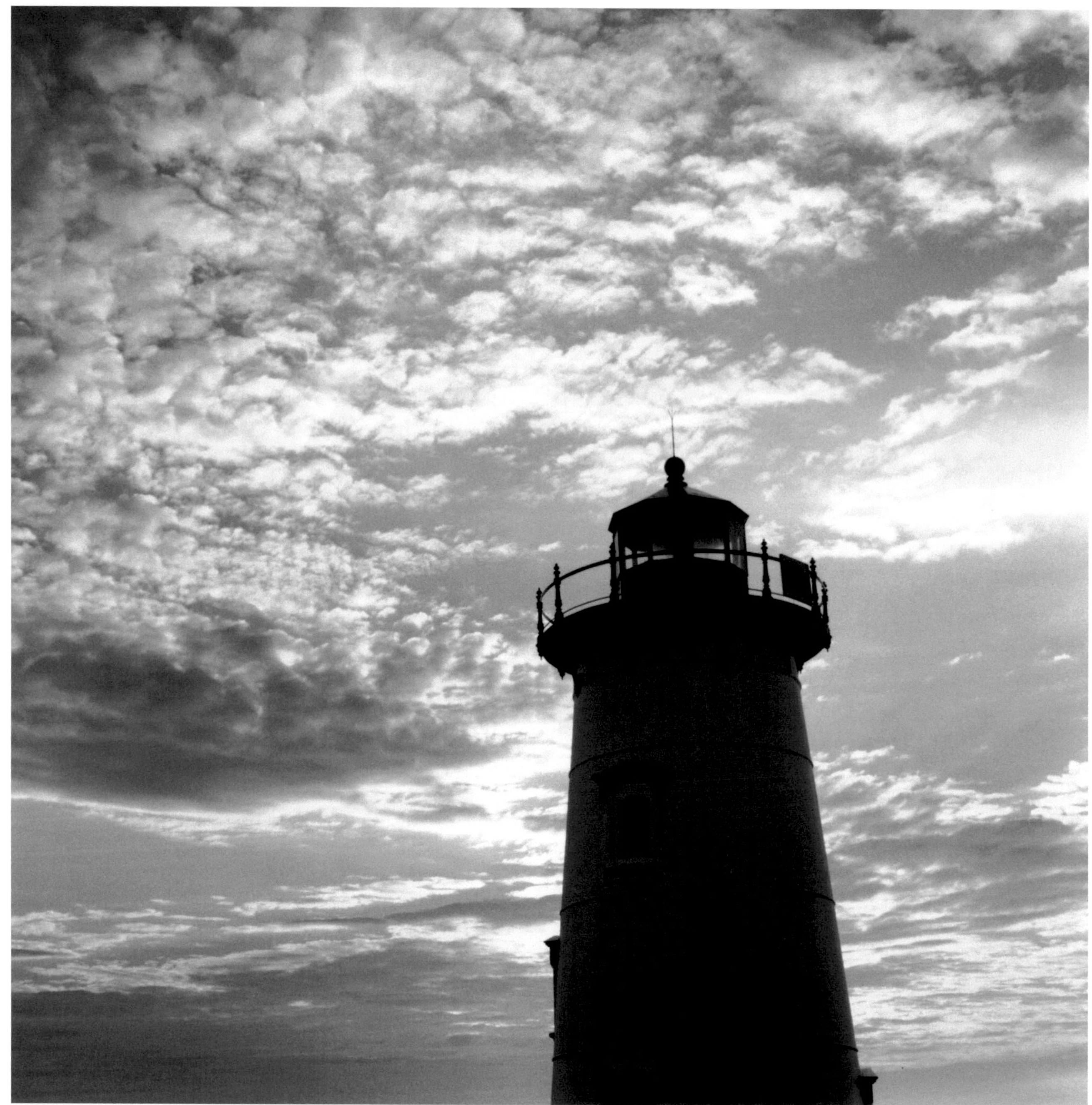

Edgartown, 1998

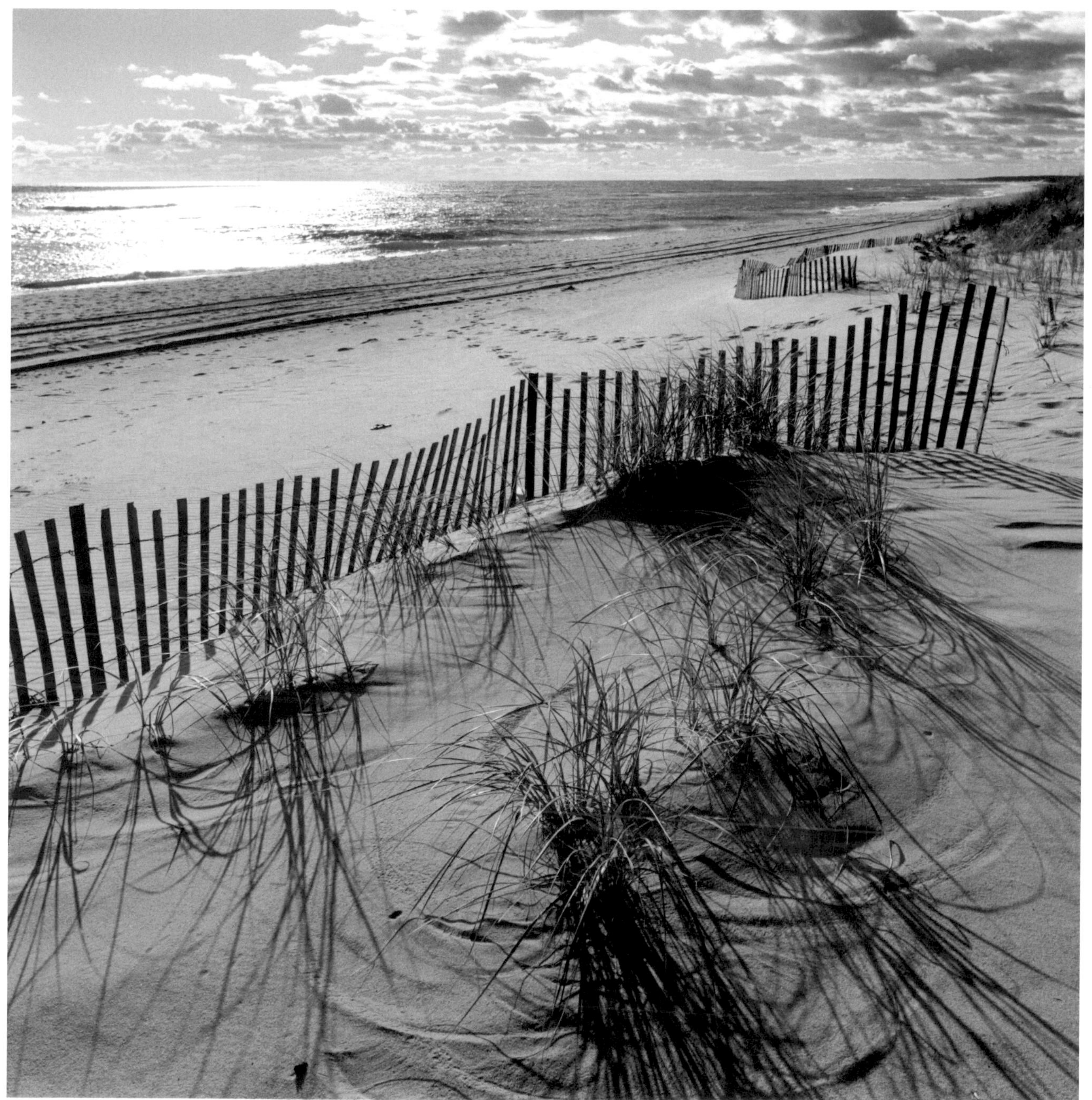

South Beach, 2006

53

E.E. CUMMINGS

may my heart always be open to little
birds who are the secrets of living
whatever they sing is better than to know
and if men should not hear them men are old

may my mind stroll about hungry
and fearless and thirsty and supple
for even if it's Sunday may i be wrong
for whenever men are right they are not young

and may myself do nothing usefully
and love yourself so more than truly
there's never been quite such a fool who could fail
pulling all the sky over him with one smile

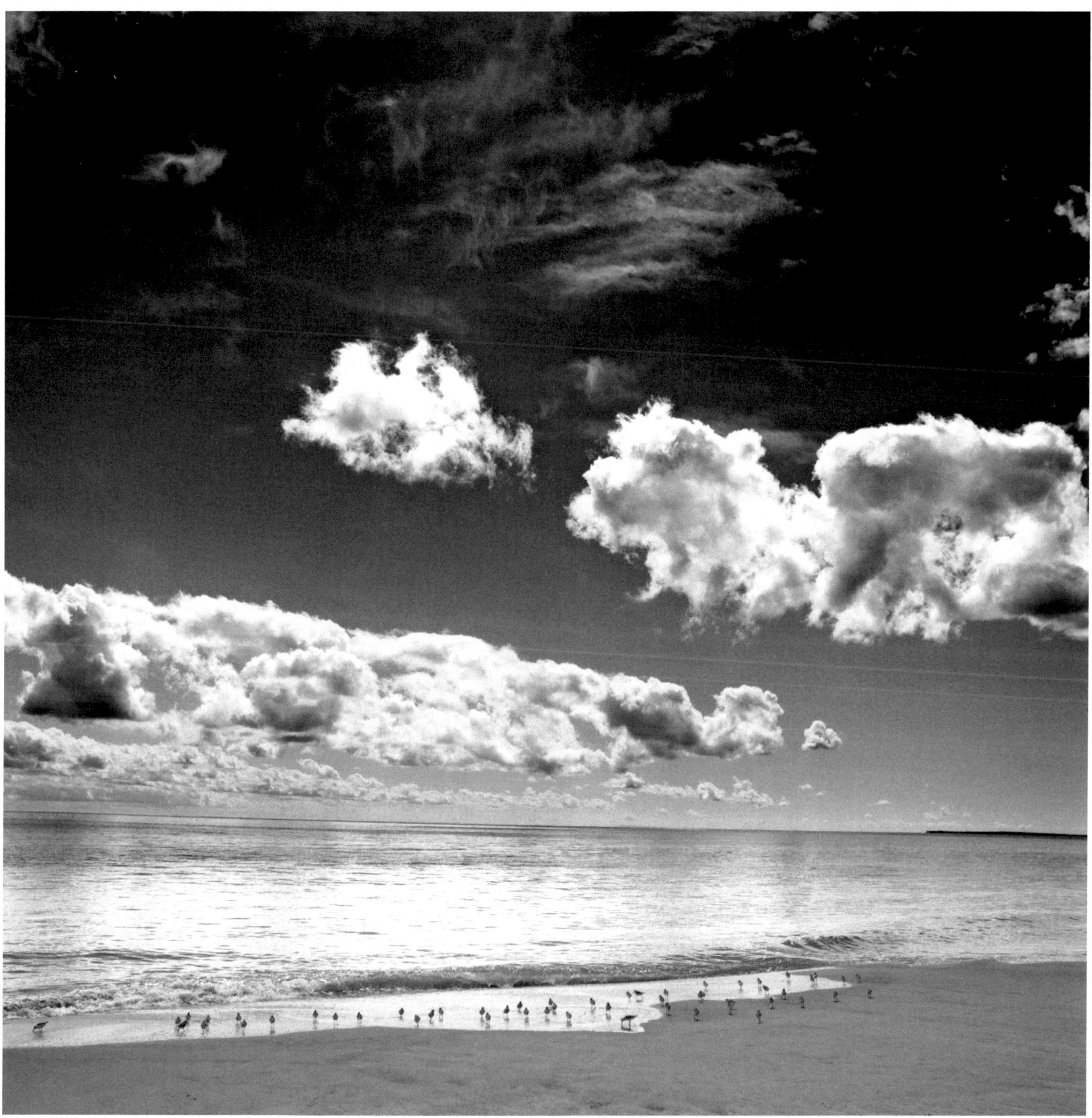

Chilmark Pond Land Bank Beach, 2014

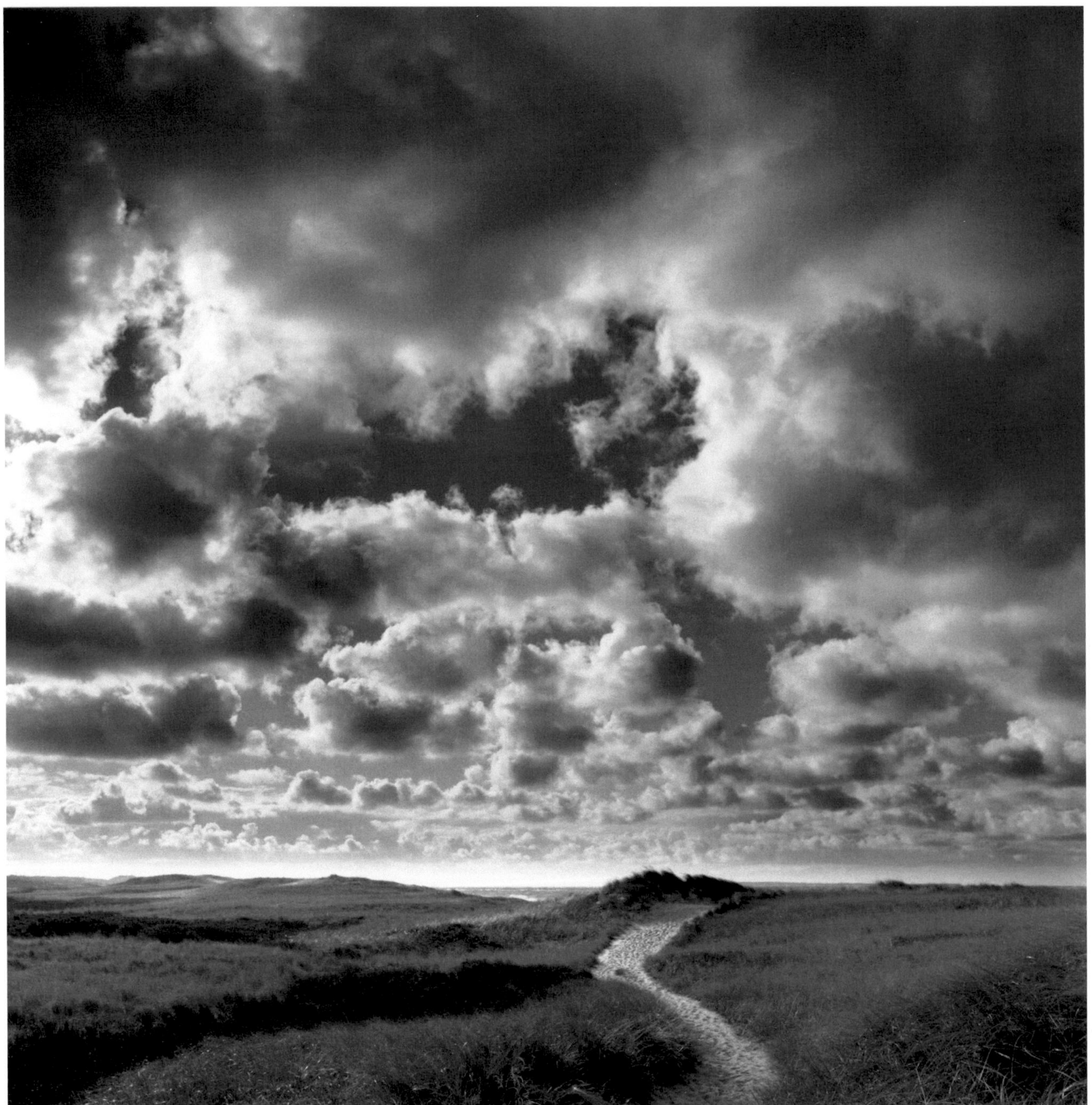

Moshup Beach, 1999

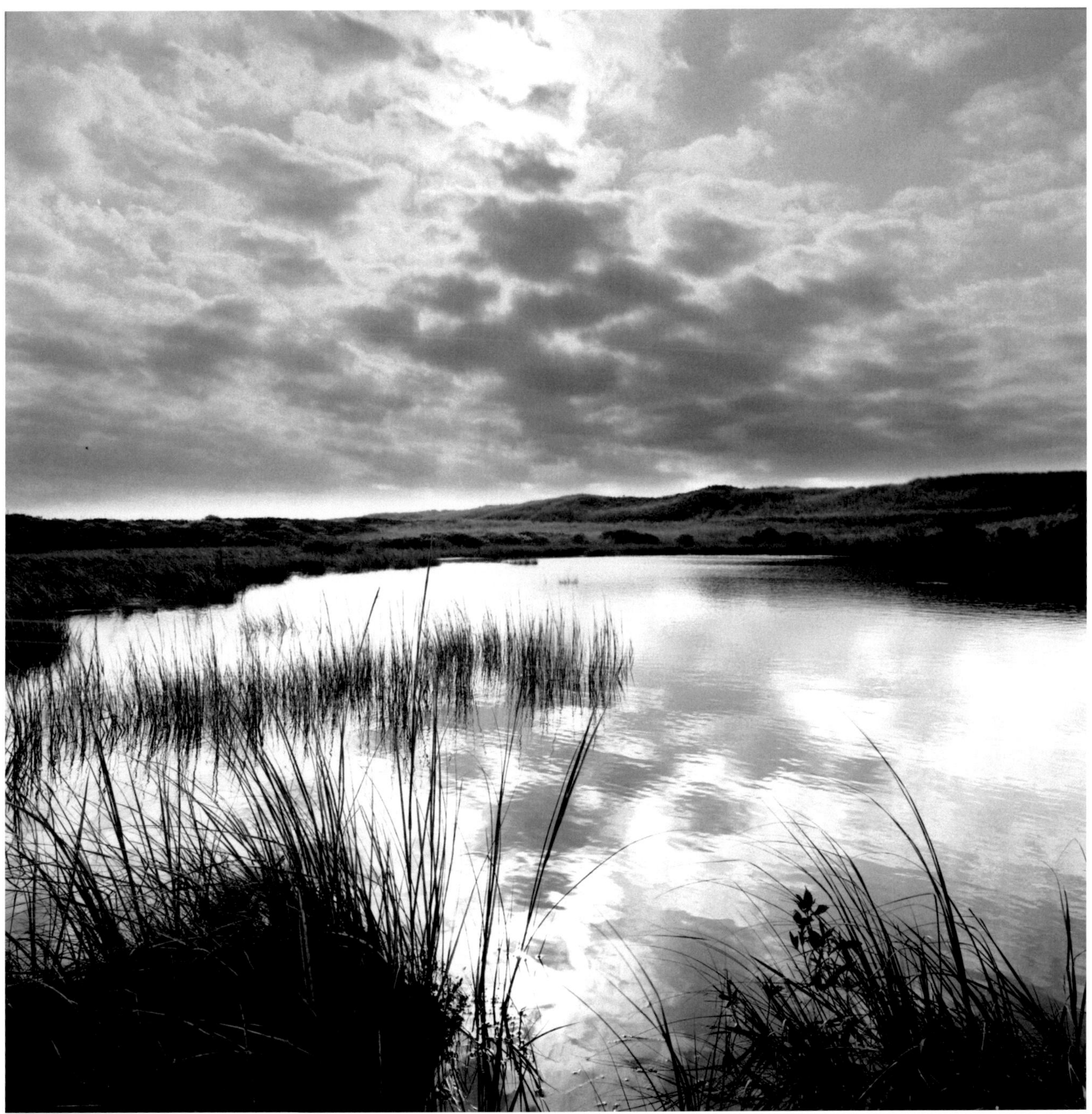

Katama Bay, 2006

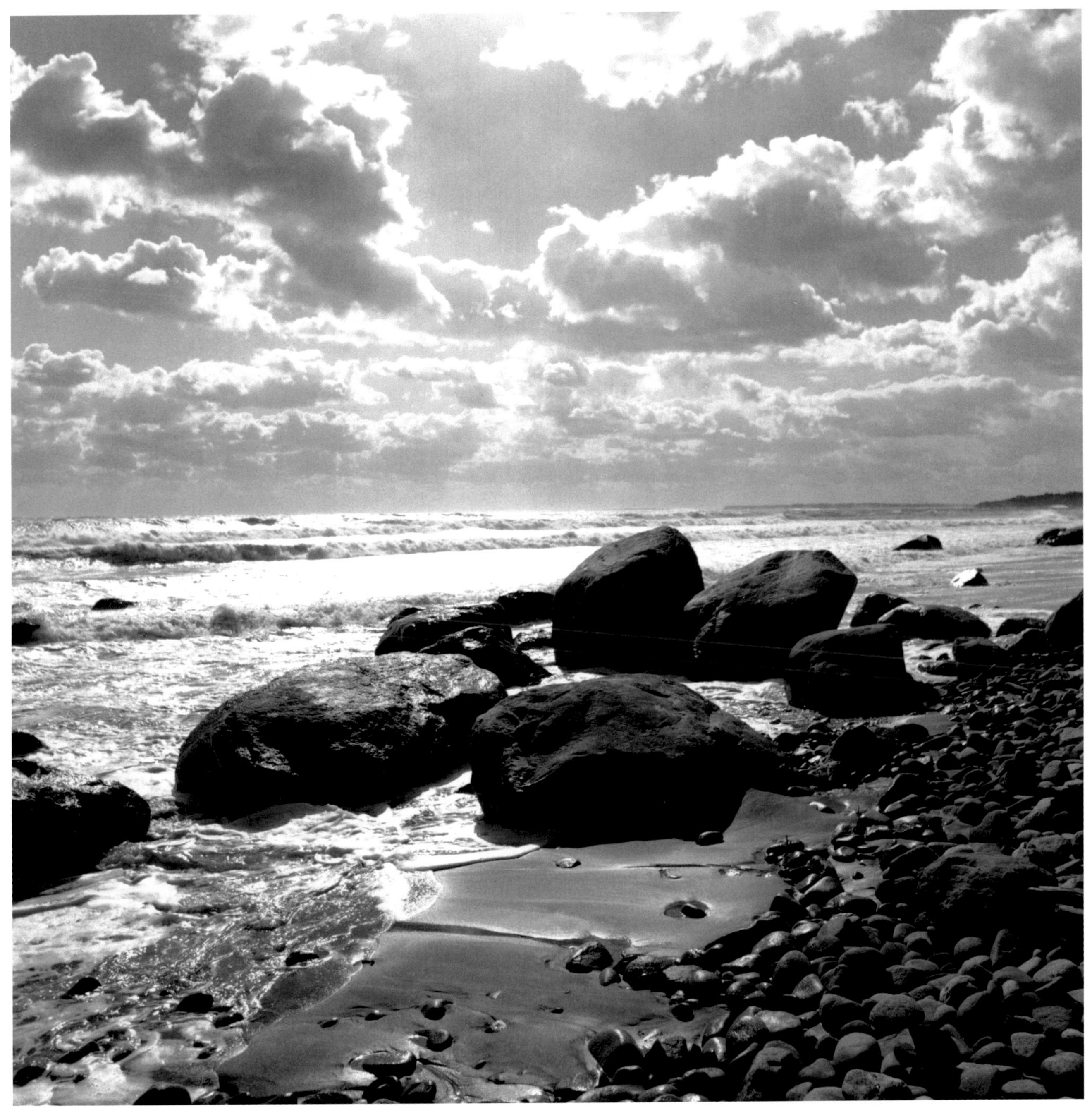

Lucy Vincent Beach, 2006

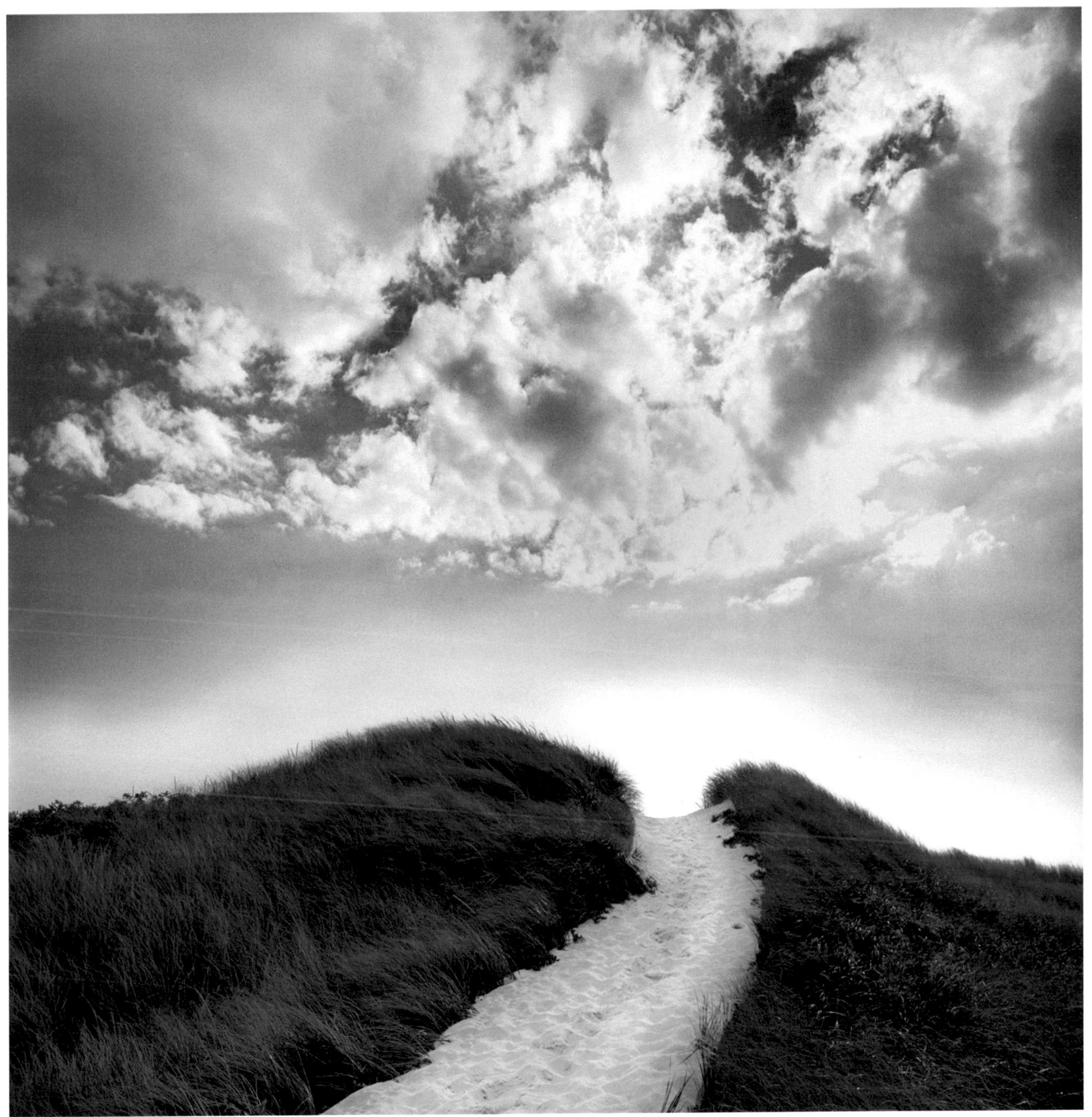

Philbin Beach, 2000

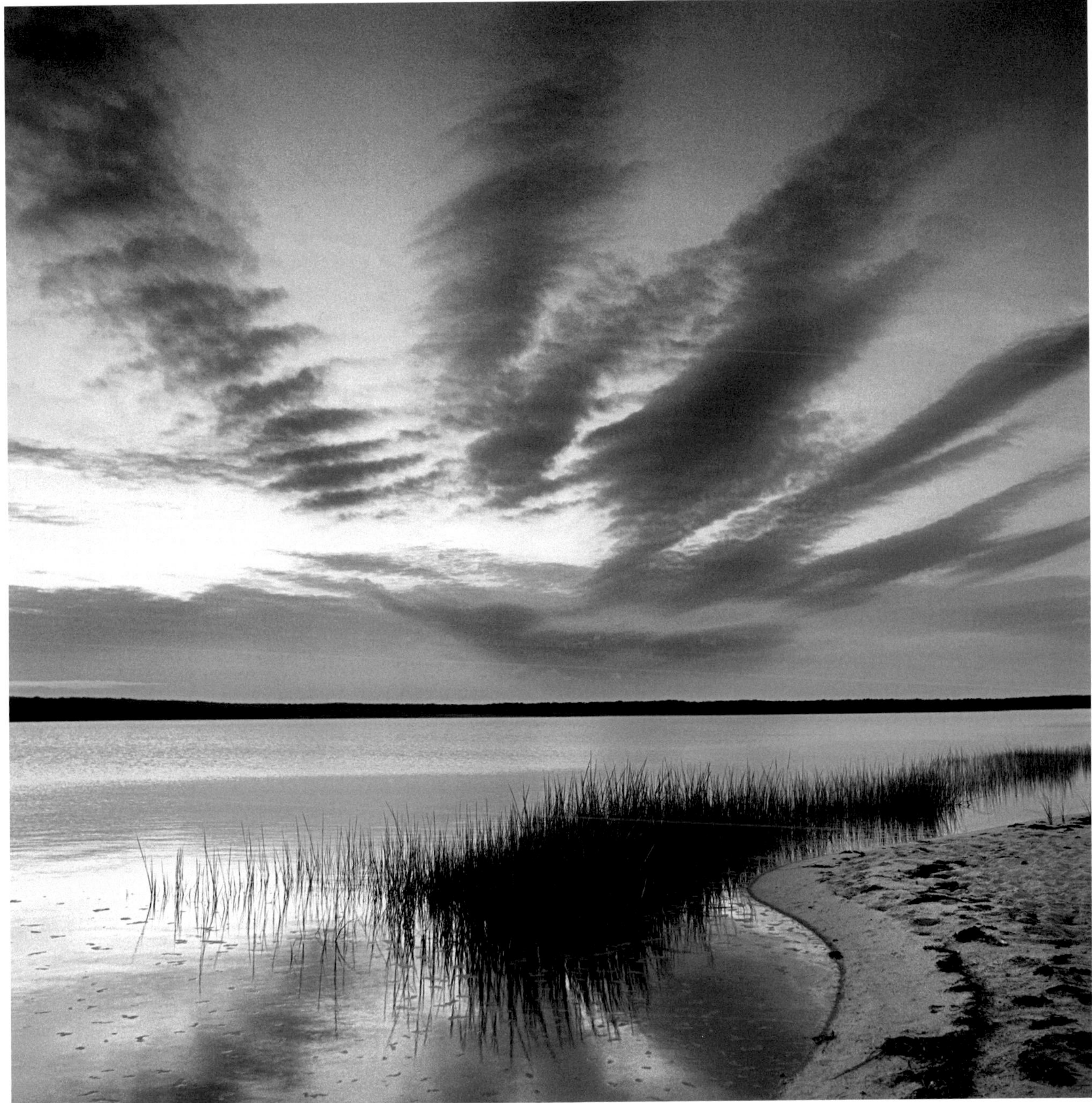

Pocha Pond, 1998

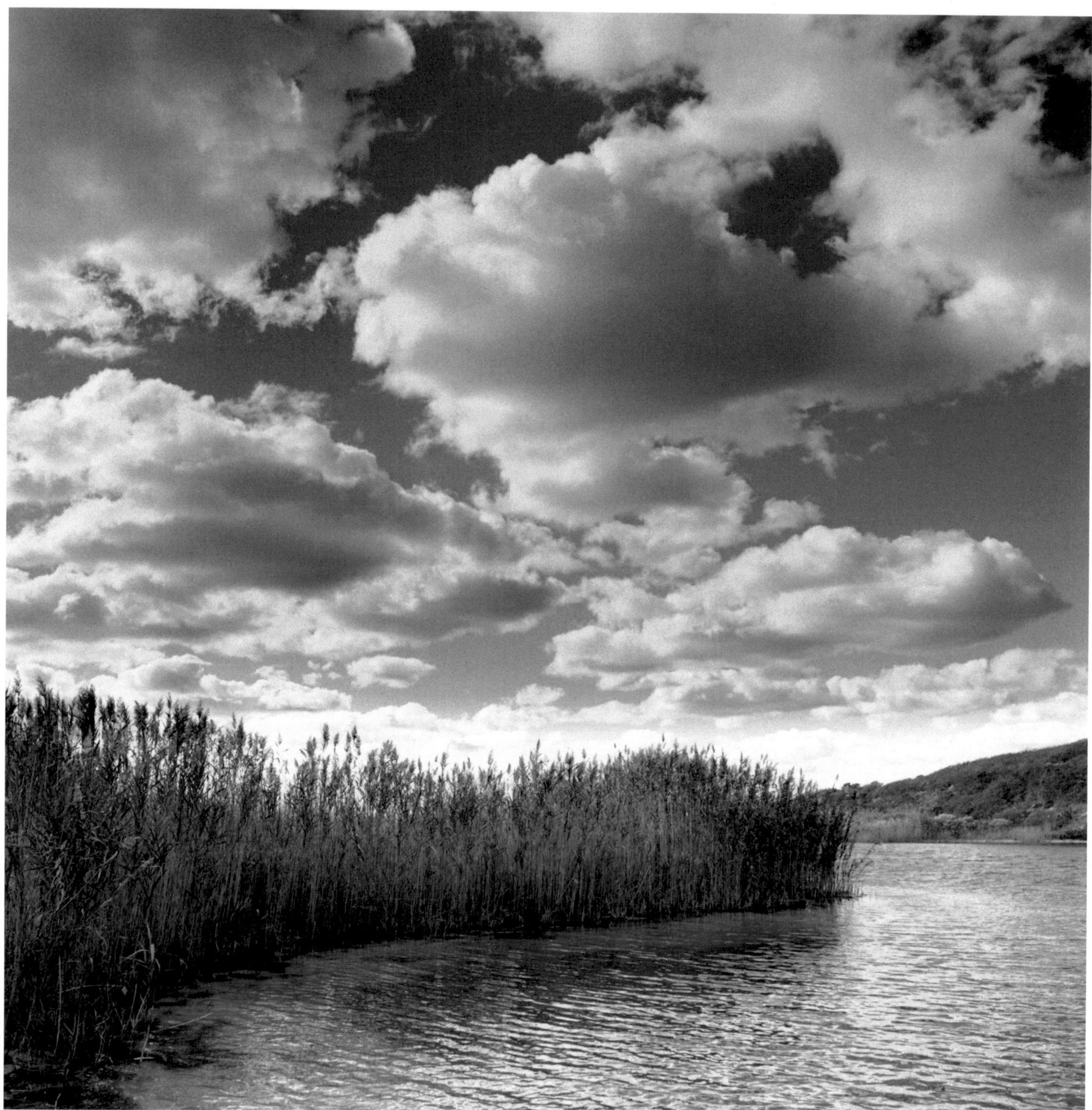

Edgartown Great Pond, 2006

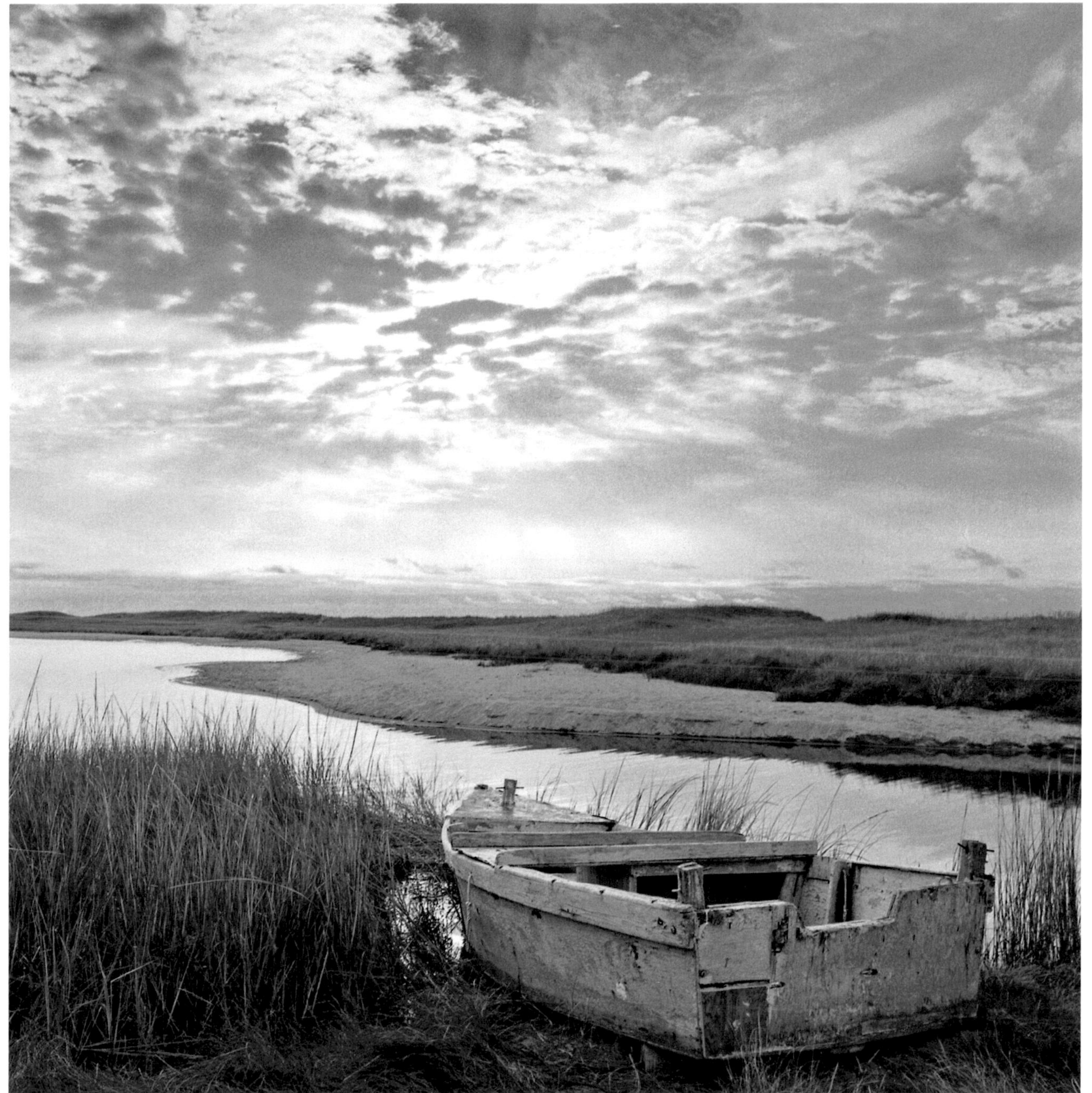

Tisbury Great Pond, 2000

CRANE

DAVID YEZZI

Paper creased is
with a touch
made less by half,
reduced as much

again by a second
fold—so the wish
to press our designs
can diminish

what we hold.
But by your hand's
careful work,
I understand

how this unleaving
makes of what's before
something finer
and finally more.

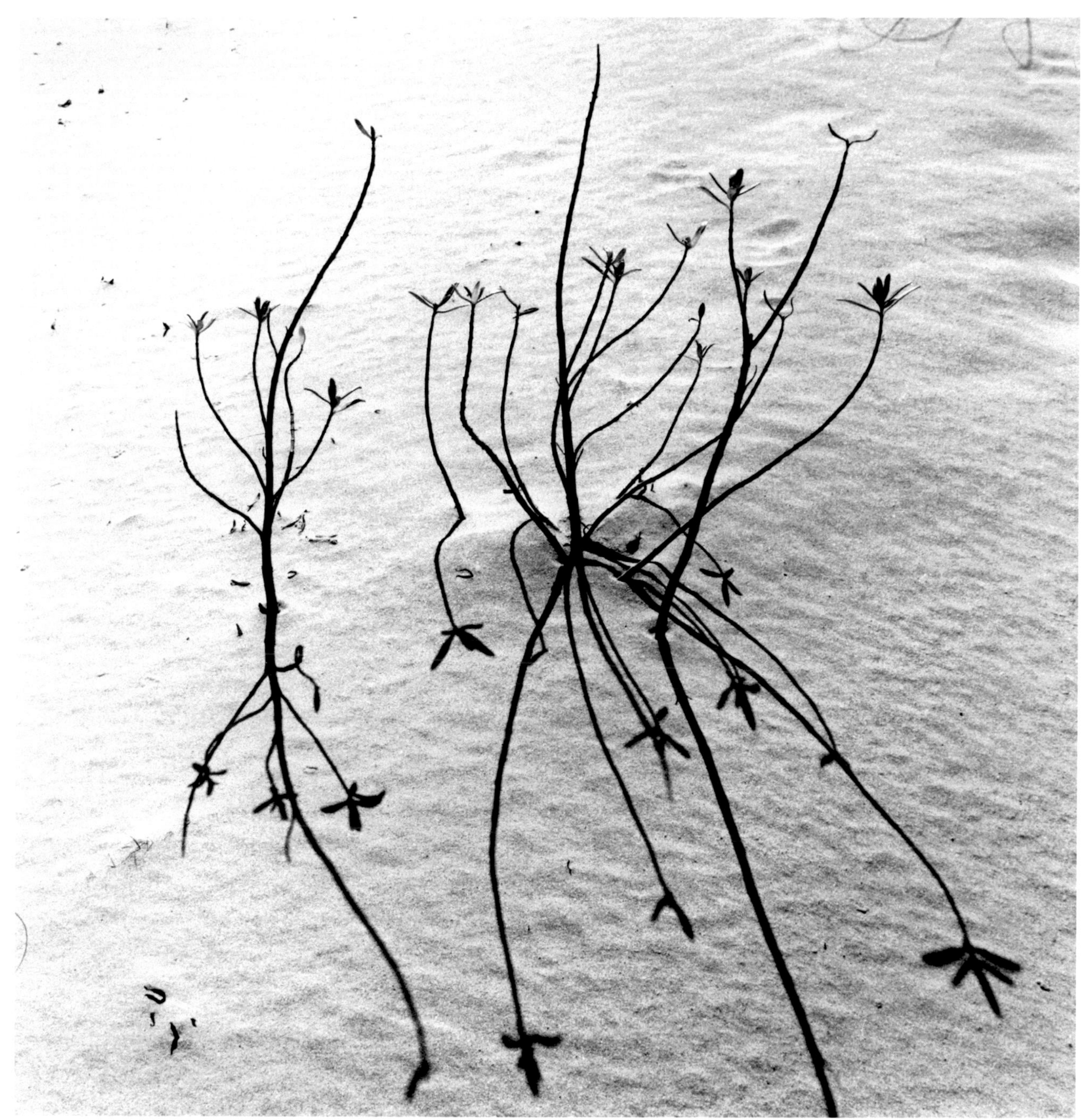

Long Point, 2012

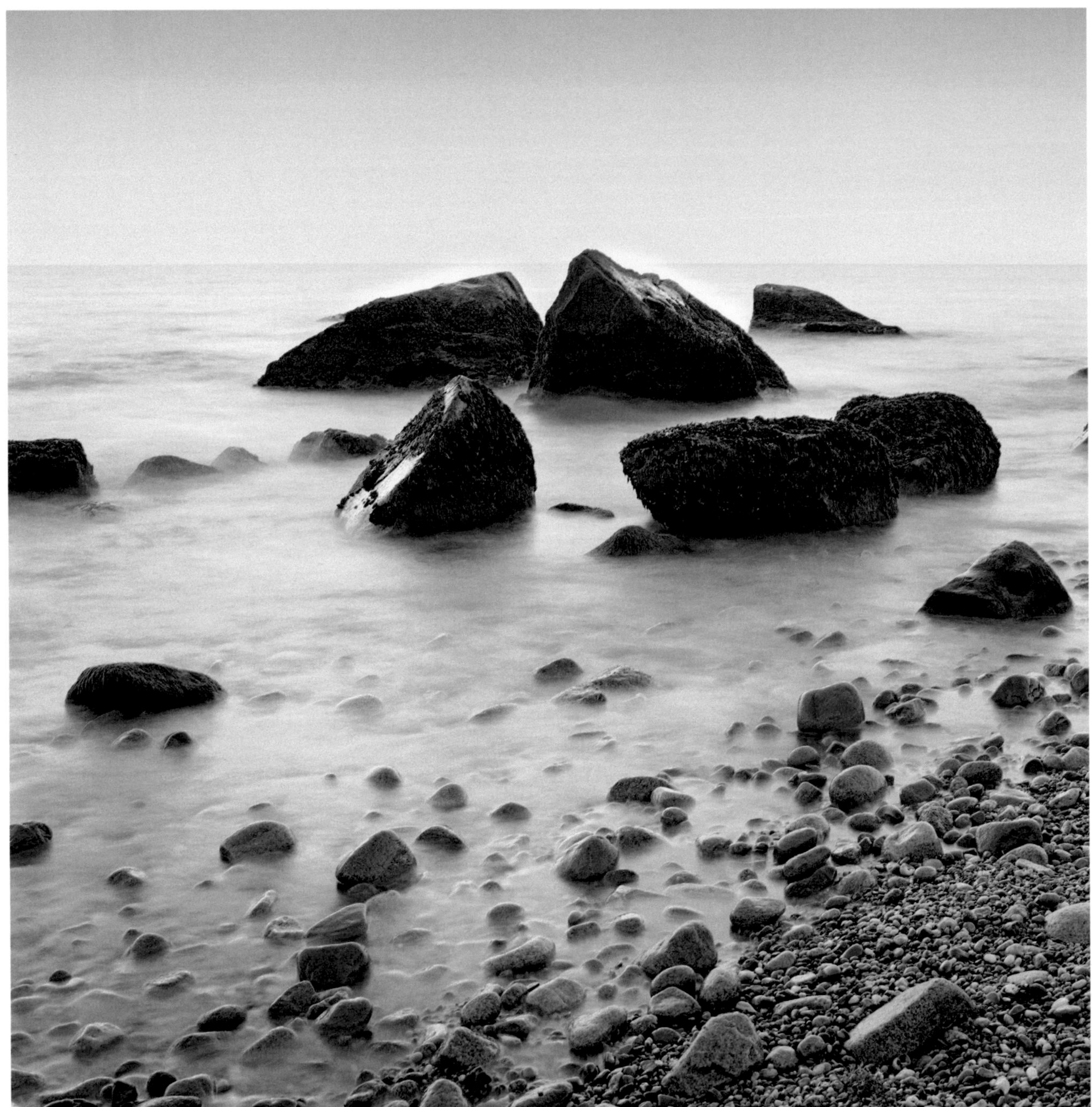

Philbin Beach, 1999

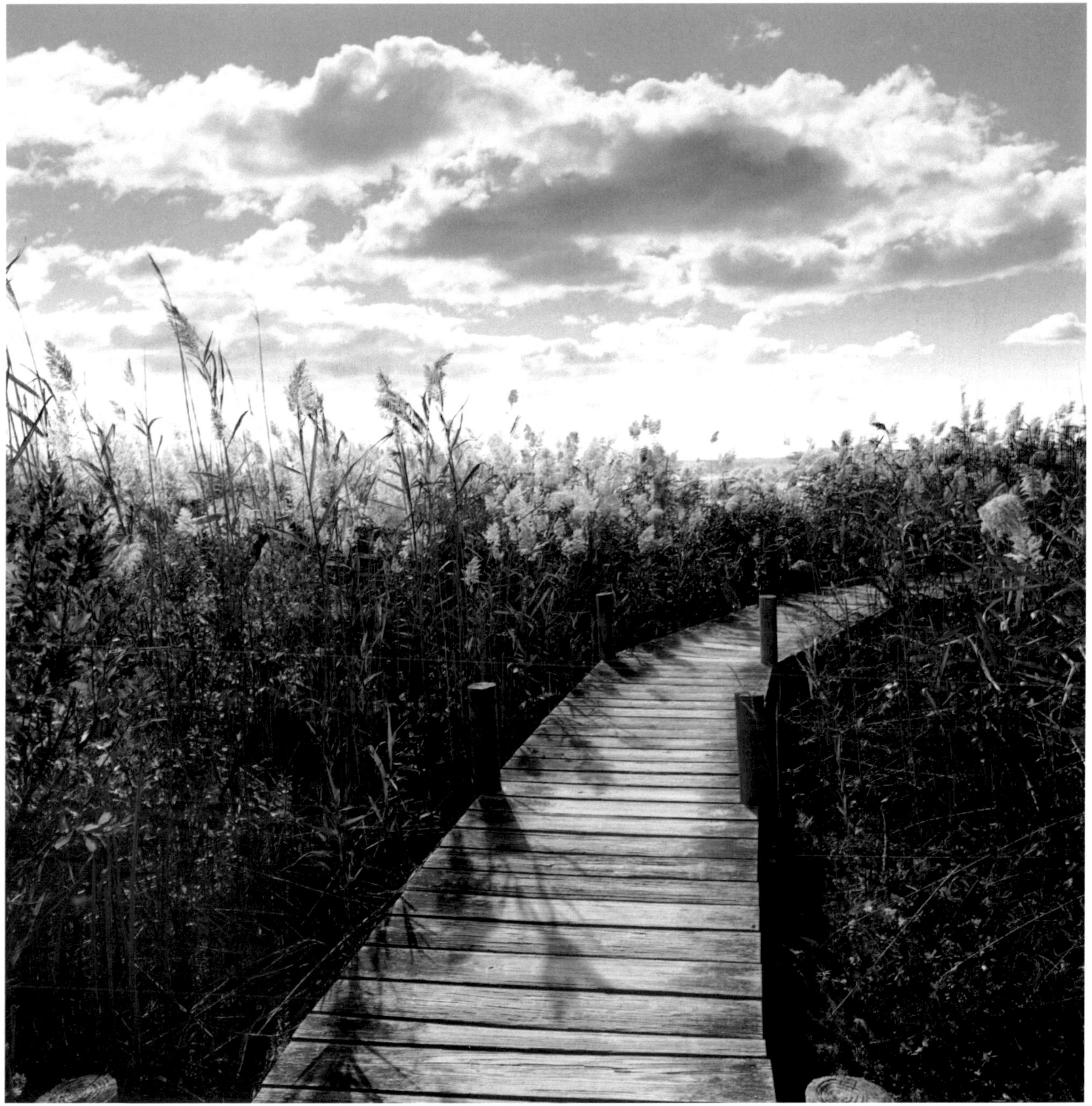

Wasque, 2006

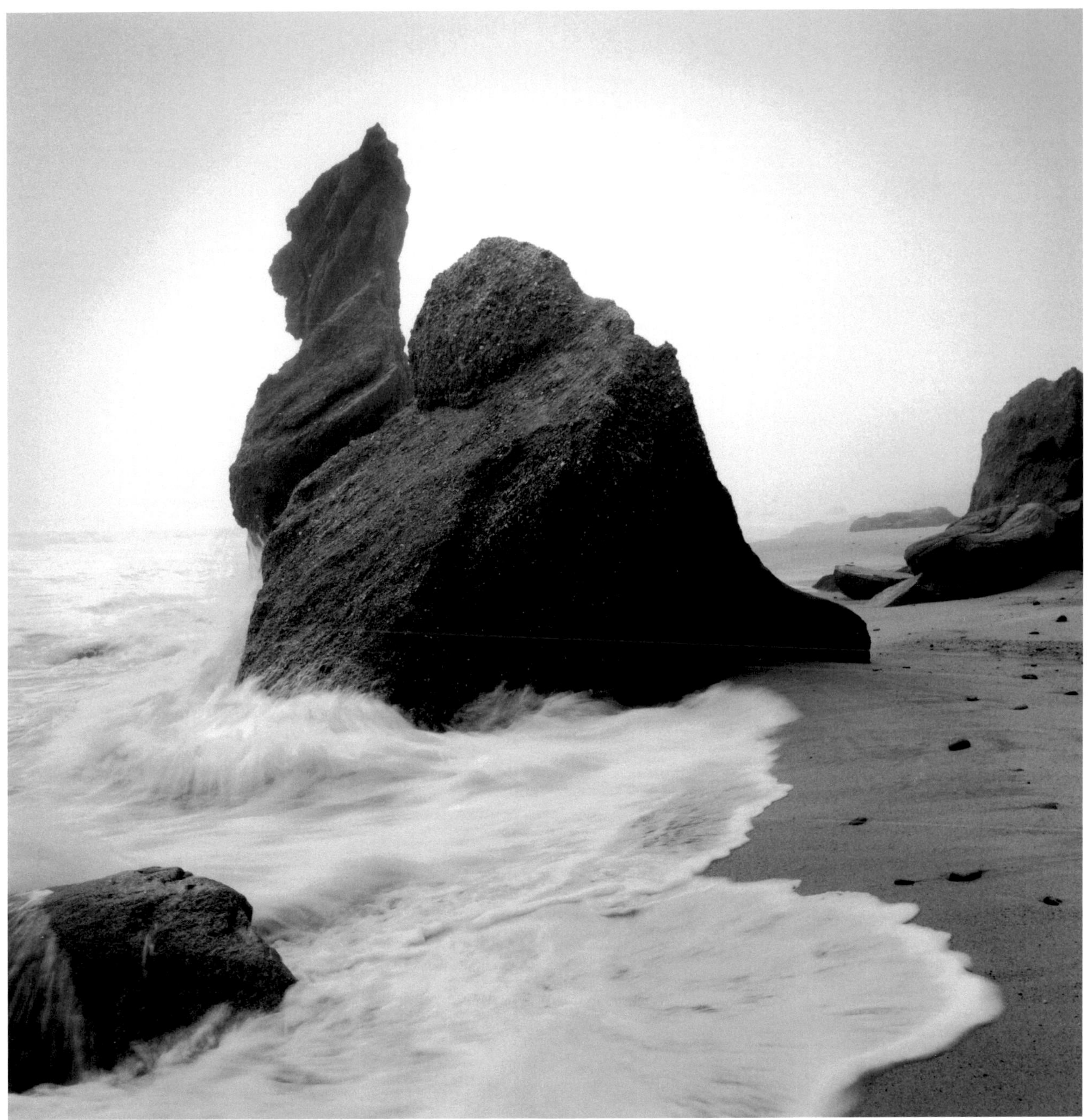
Lucy Vincent Beach, 2017

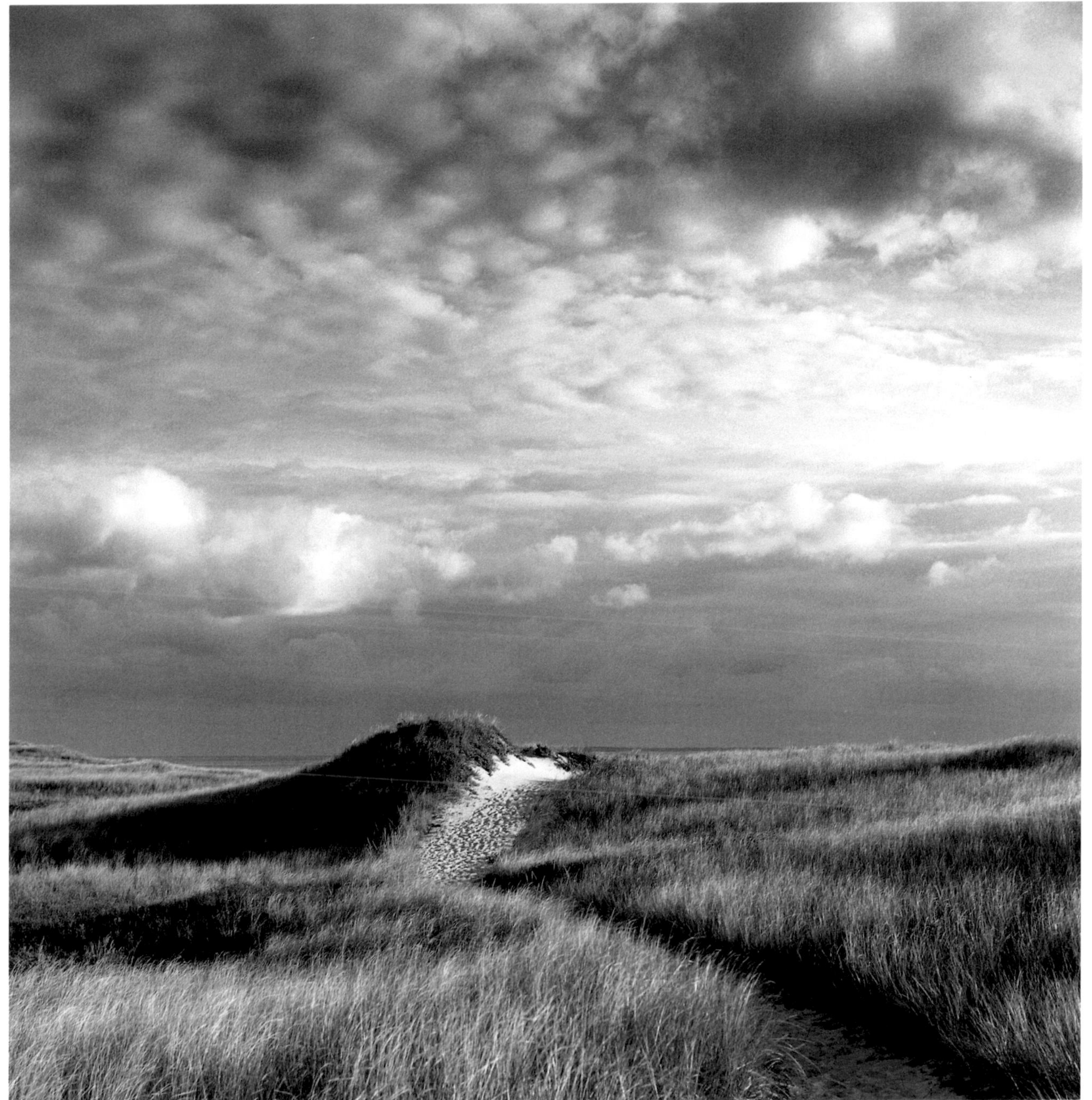

Moshup Beach, 2004

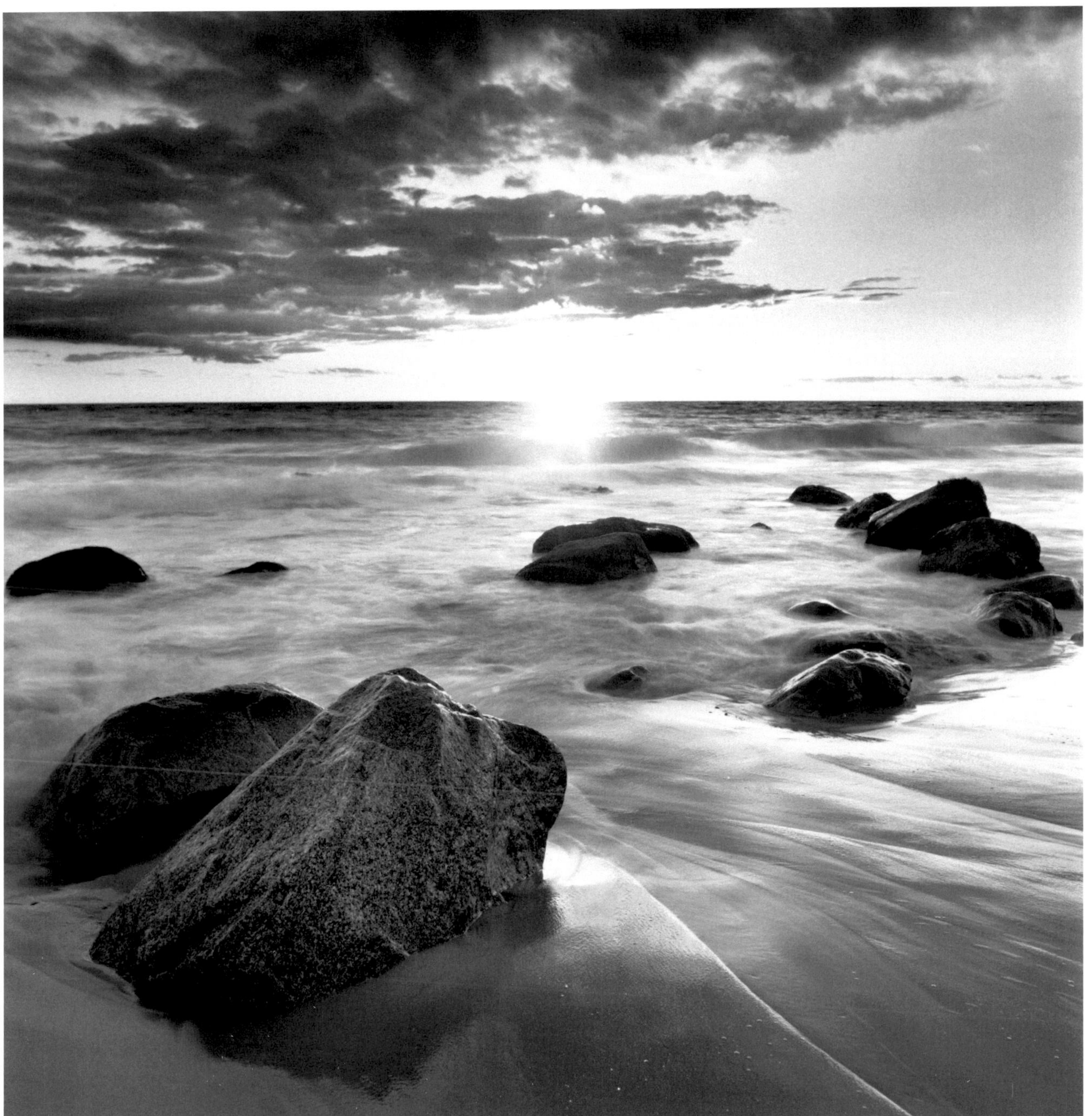

Long Beach, 2000

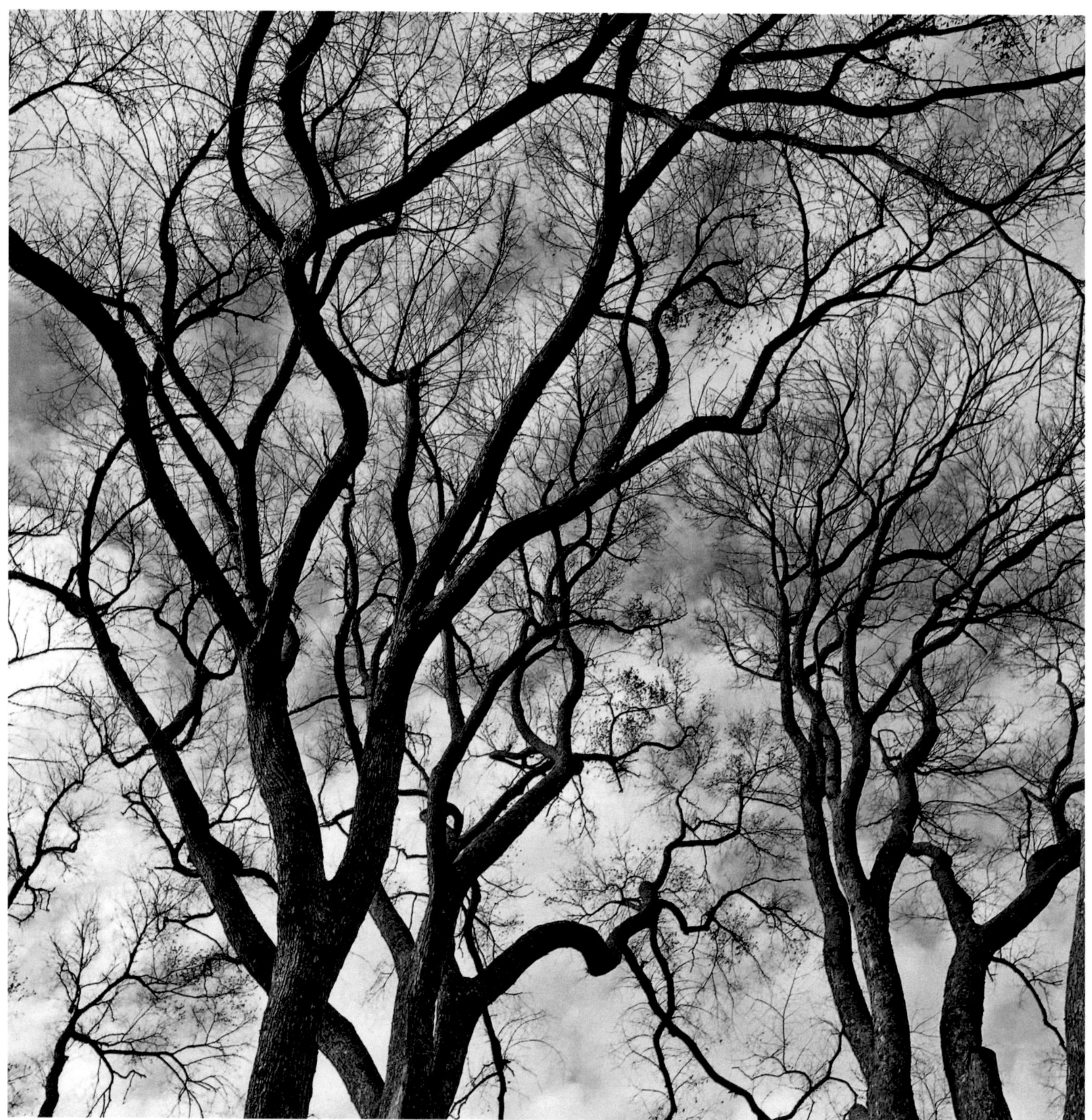
Chilmark, 1999

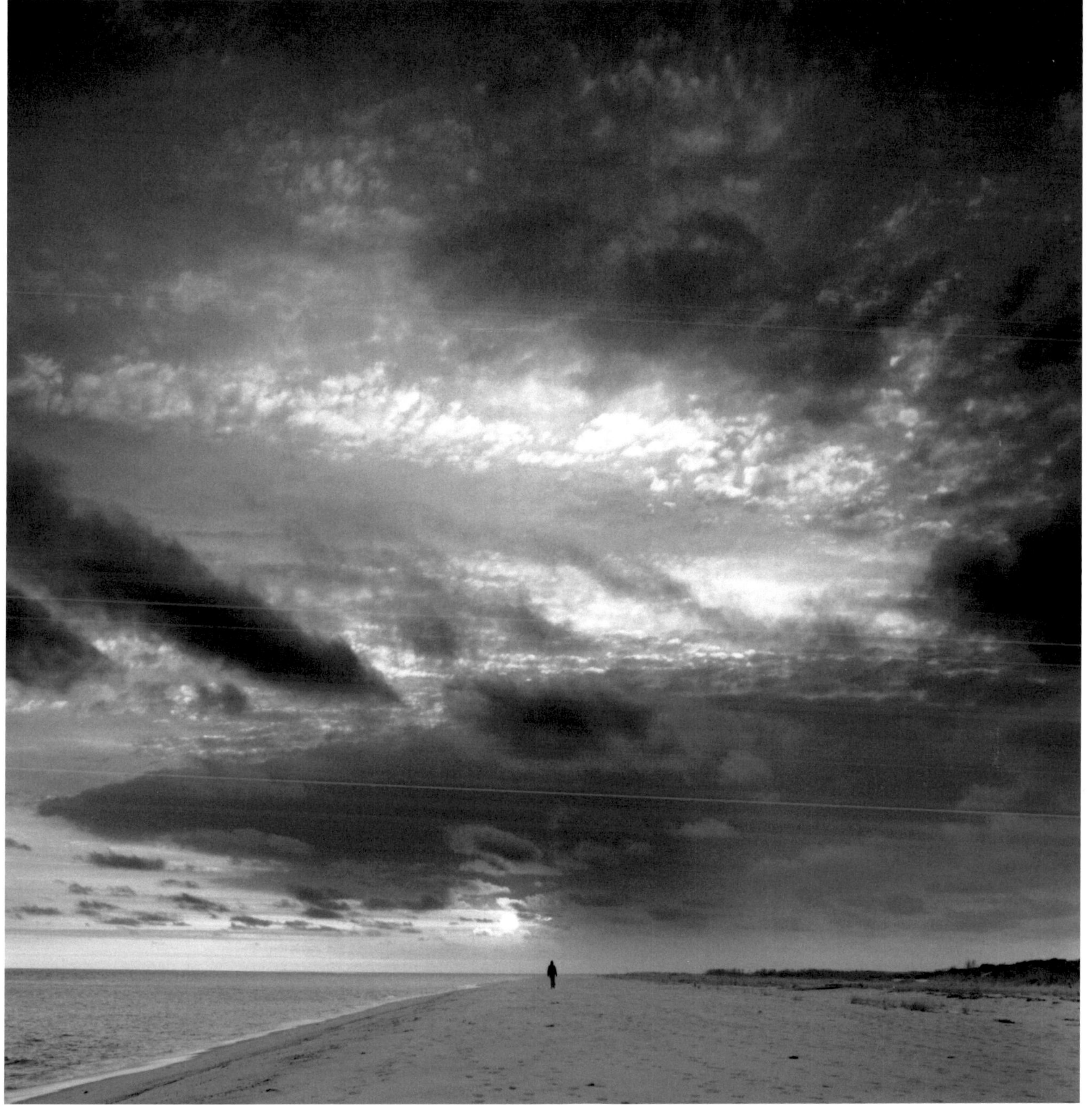

East Beach, 2004

THE PEACE OF WILD THINGS

WENDELL BERRY

When despair for the world grows in me
and I wake in the night at the least sound
in fear of what my life and my children's lives may be,
I go and lie down where the wood drake
rests in his beauty on the water, and the great heron feeds.
I come into the peace of wild things
who do not tax their lives with forethought
of grief. I come into the presence of still water.
And I feel above me the day-blind stars
waiting with their light. For a time
I rest in the grace of the world, and am free.

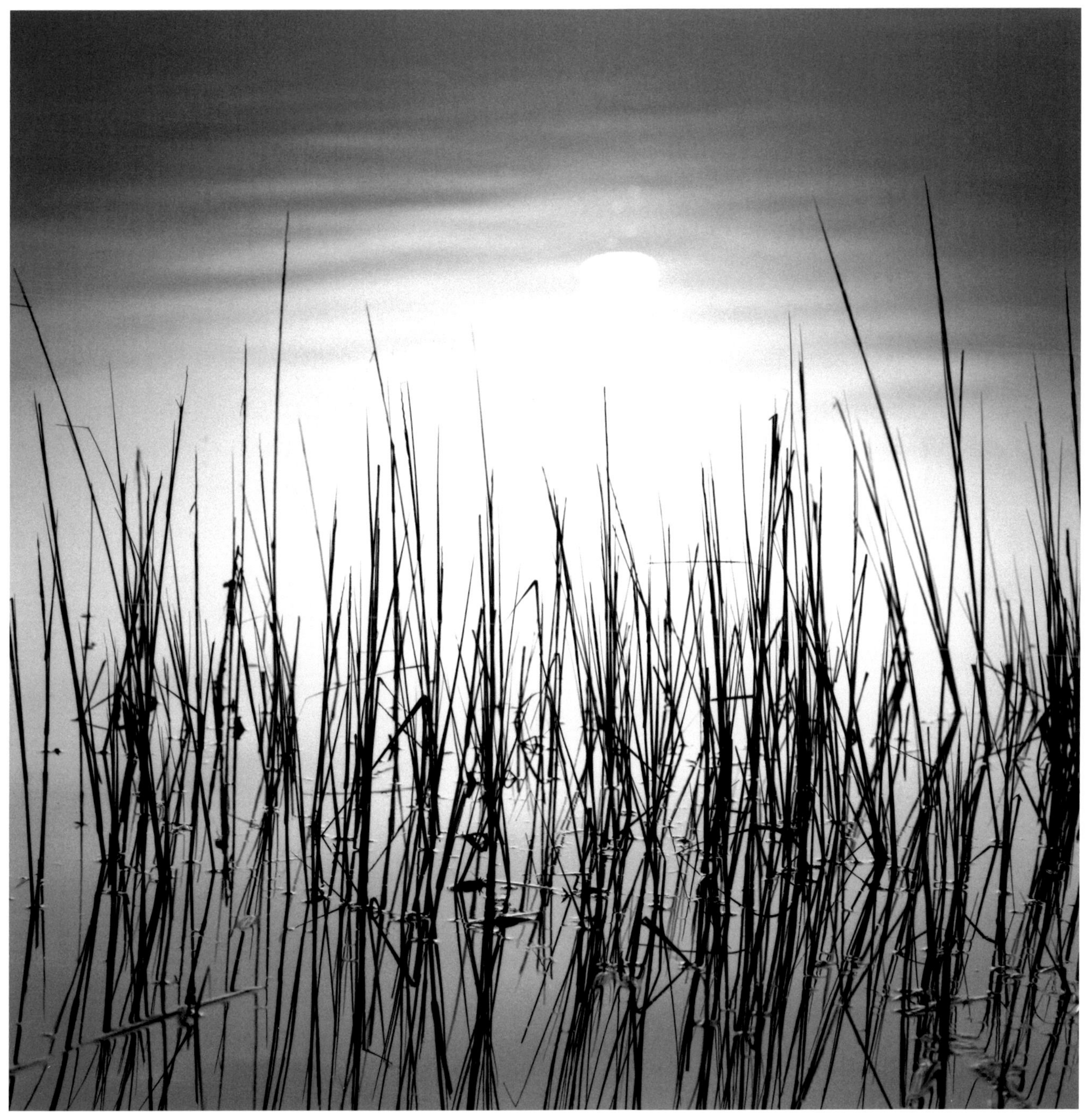

Long Pond, 2000

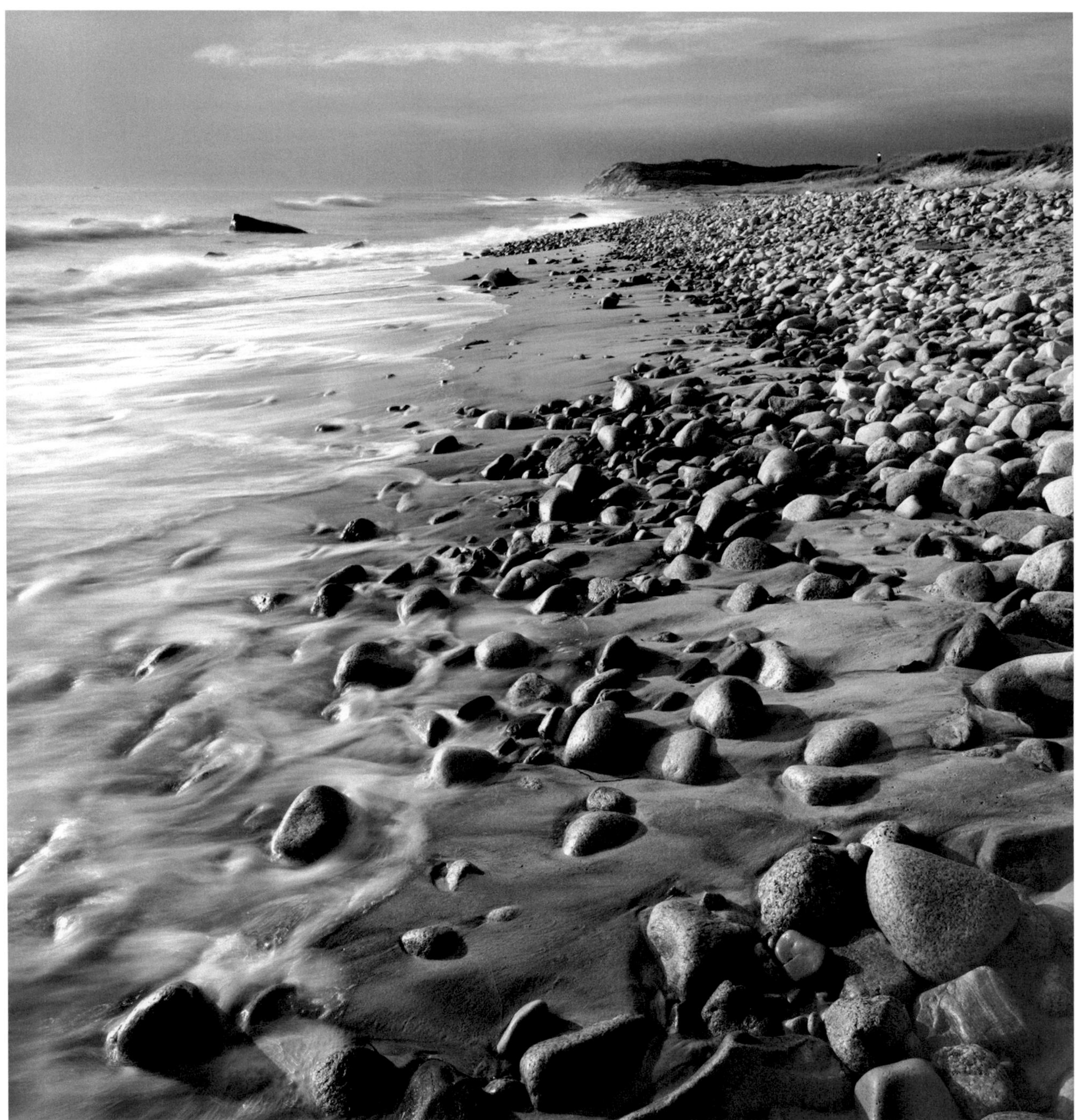

Aquinnah Beach, 1998

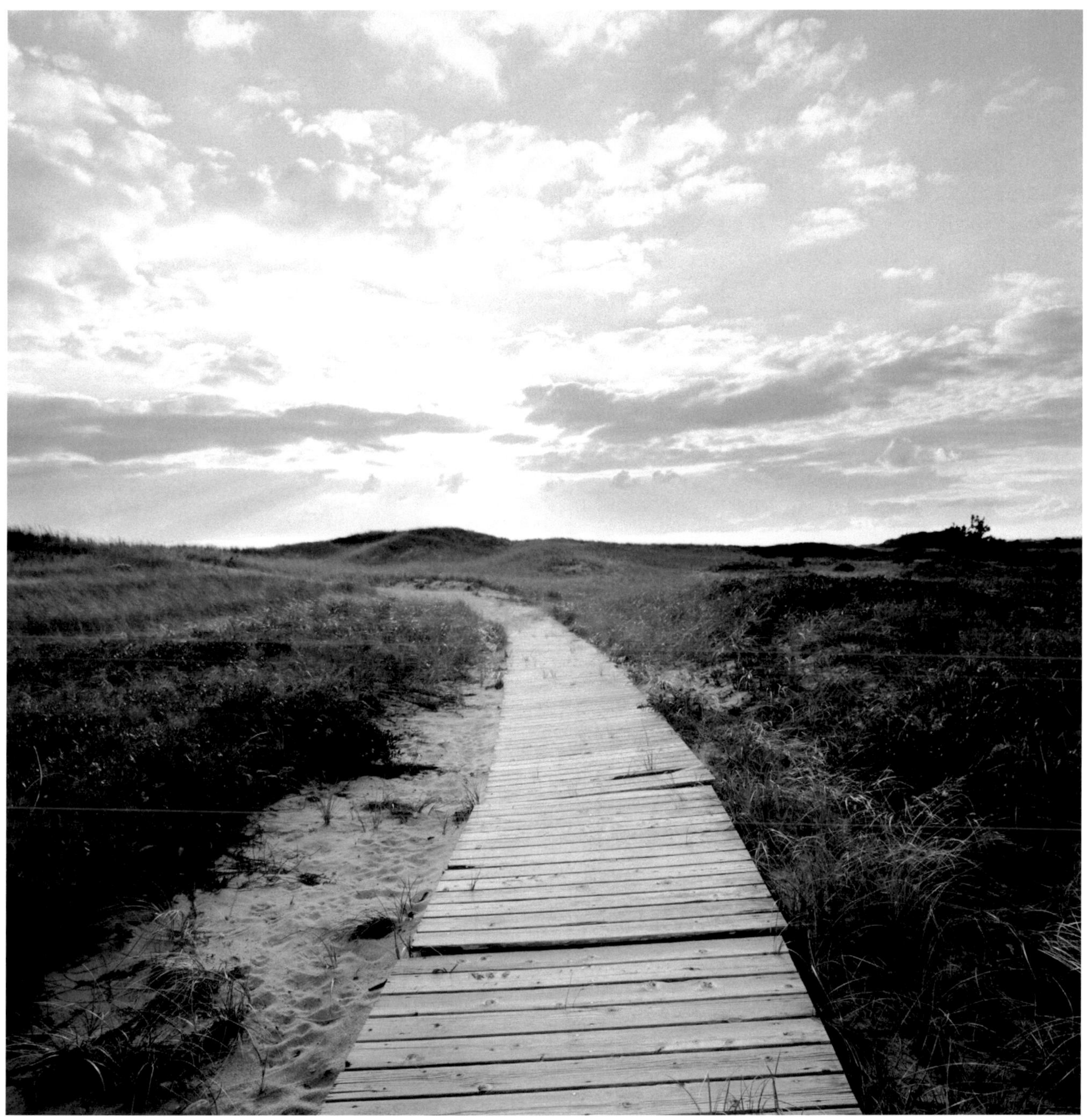

South Beach, 2006

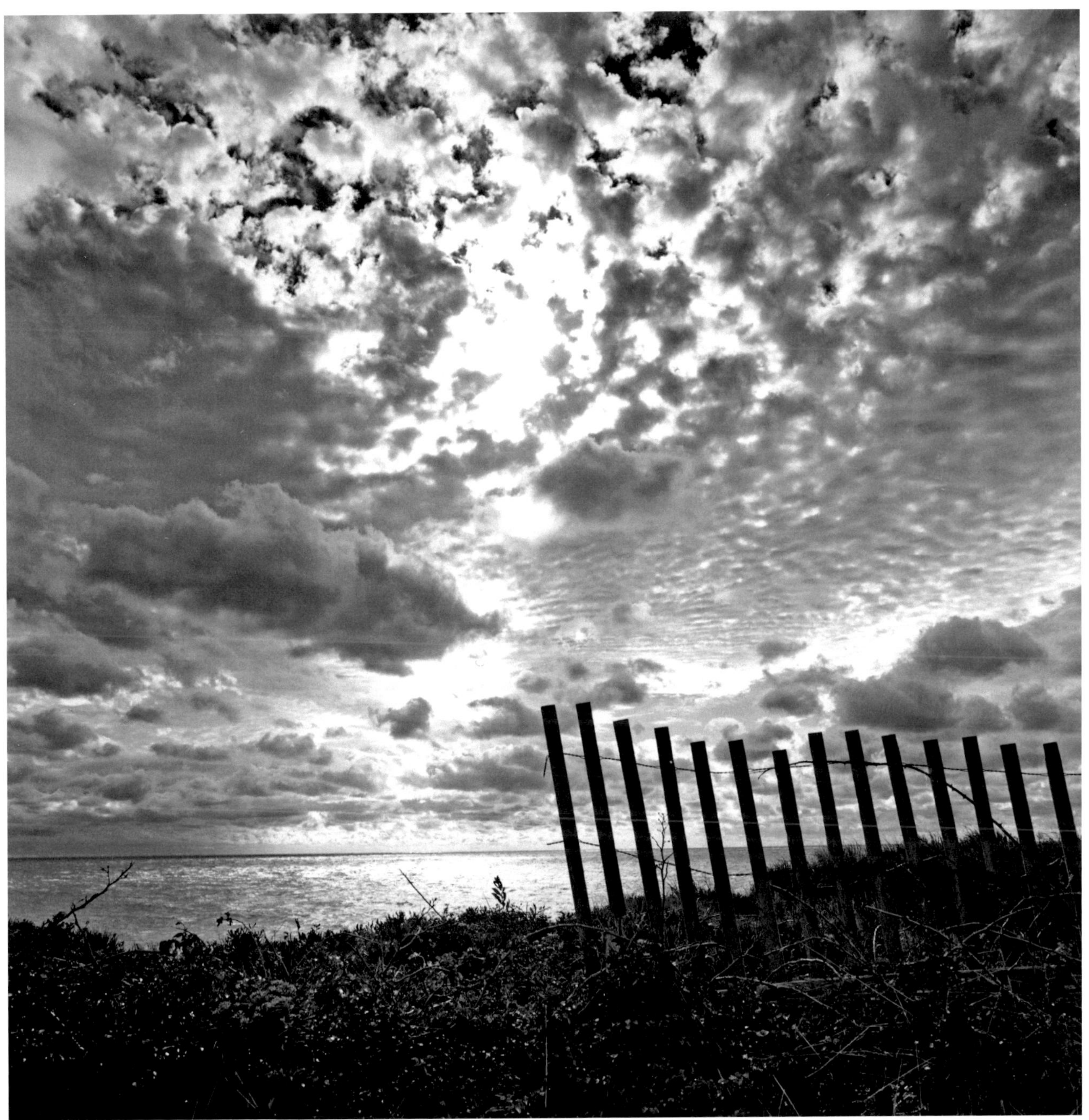

Aquinnah Headlands Preserve, 2012

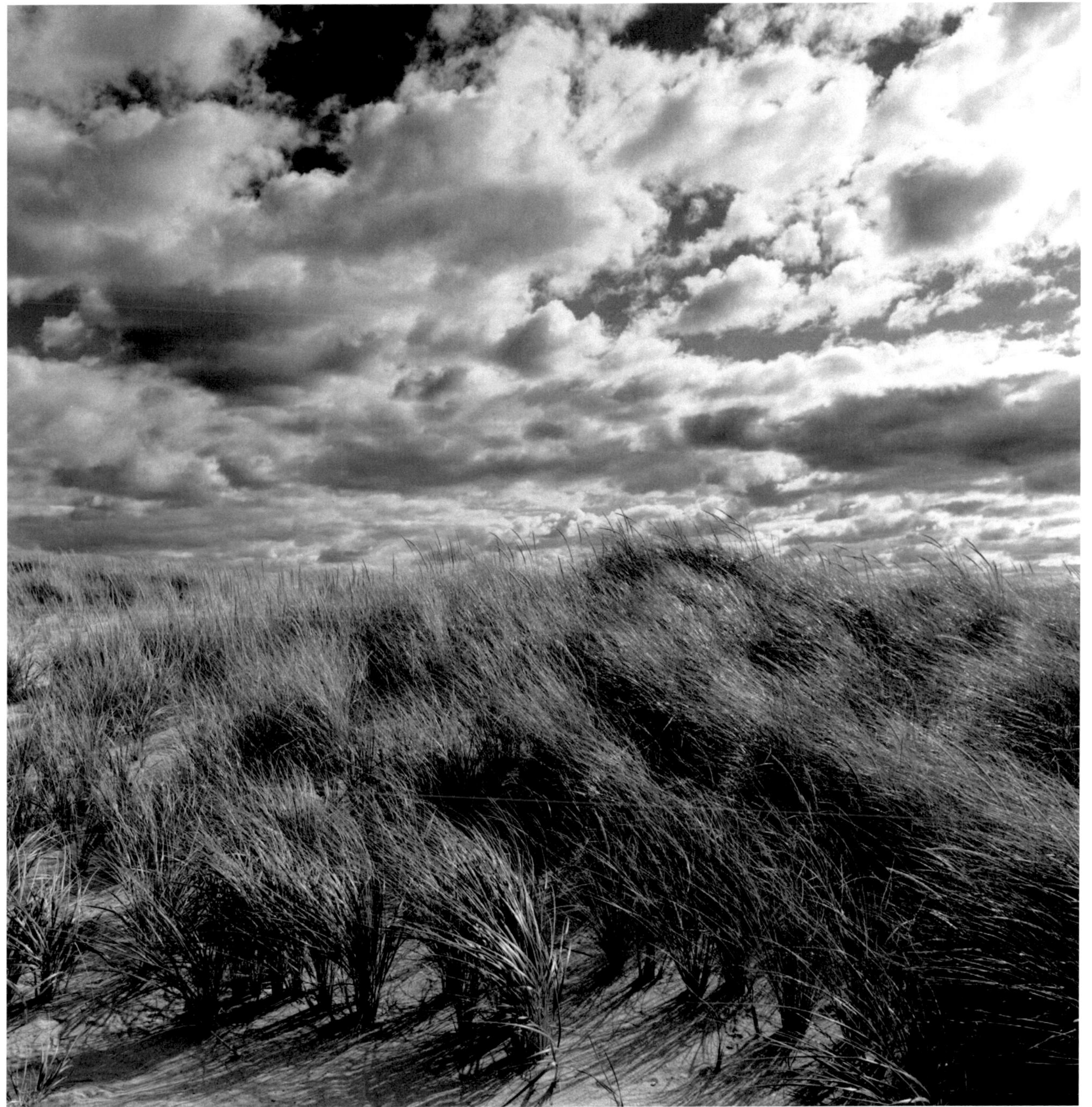

South Shore, 2006

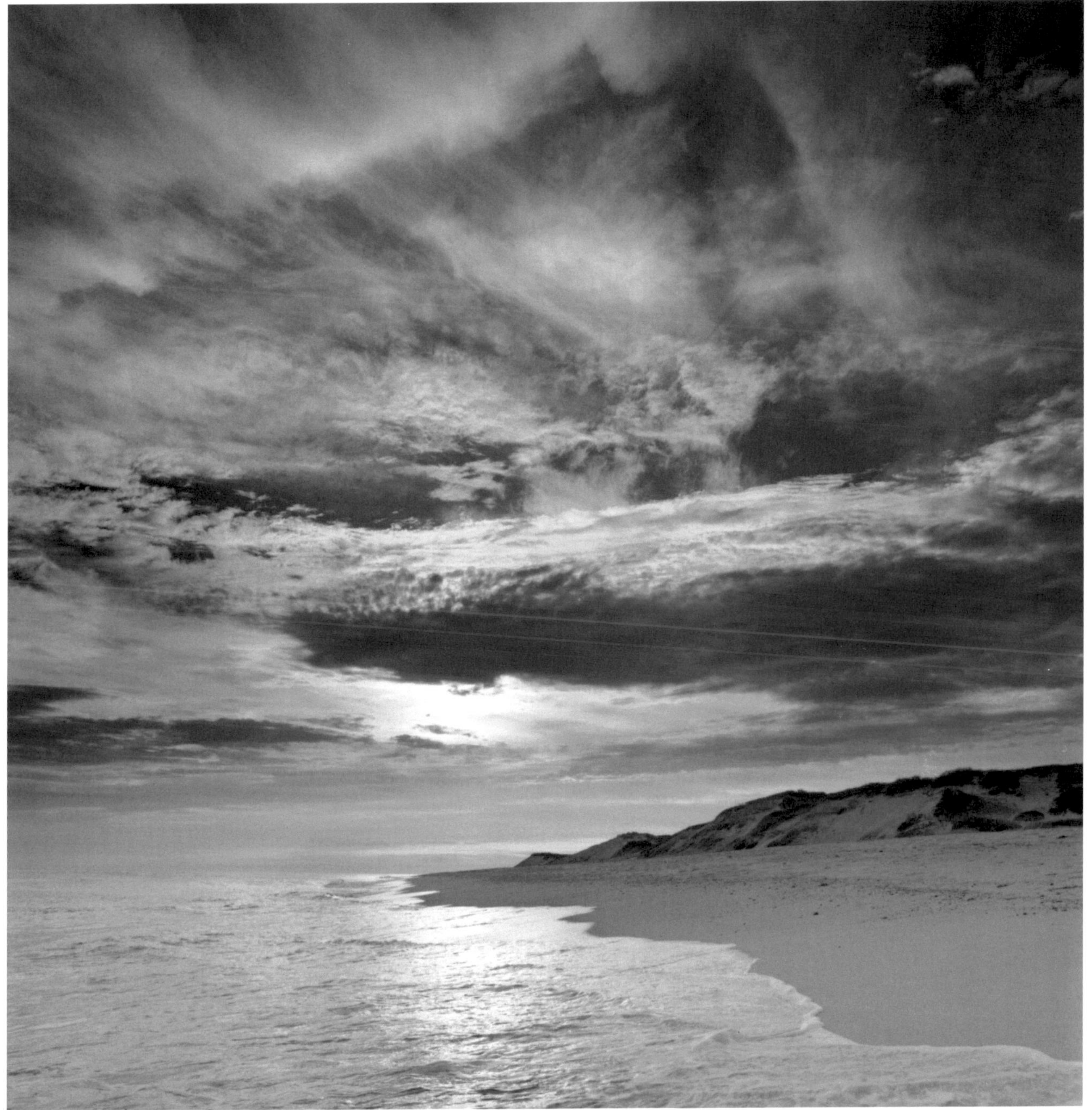

Quansoo, 2015

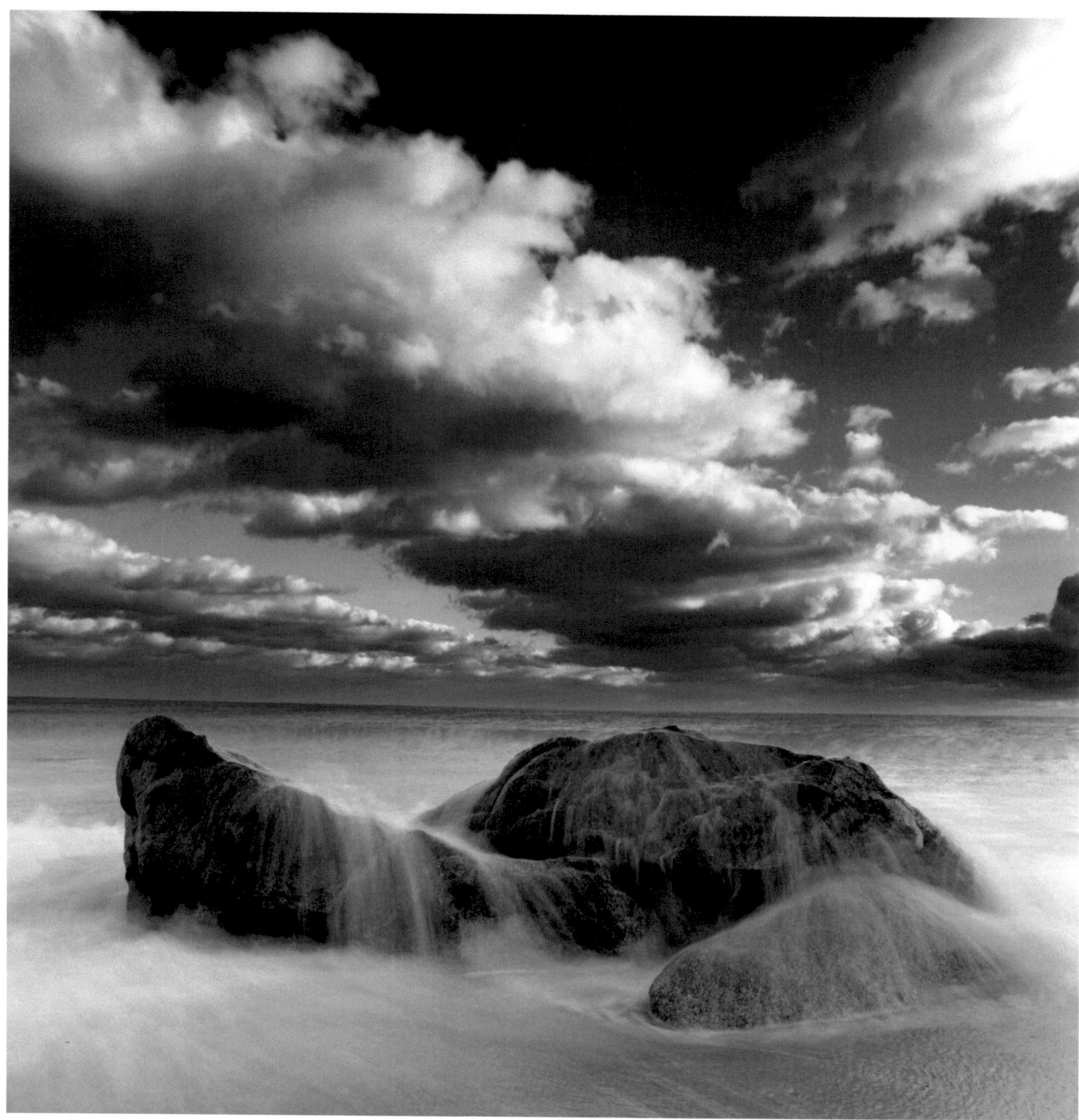

Lucy Vincent, 1999

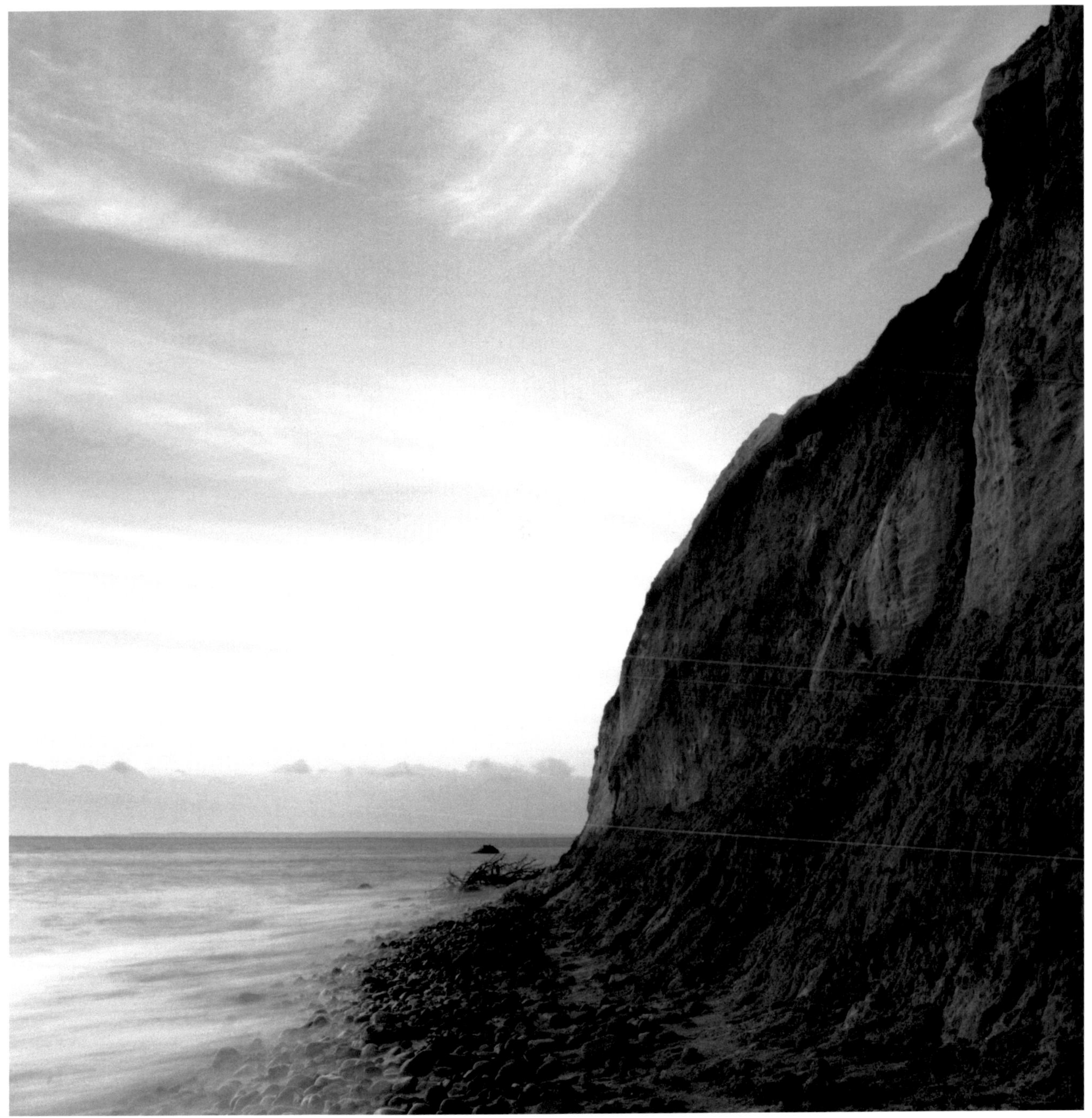

Aquinnah, 2001

Every moment of light and dark is a miracle.

—WALT WHITMAN

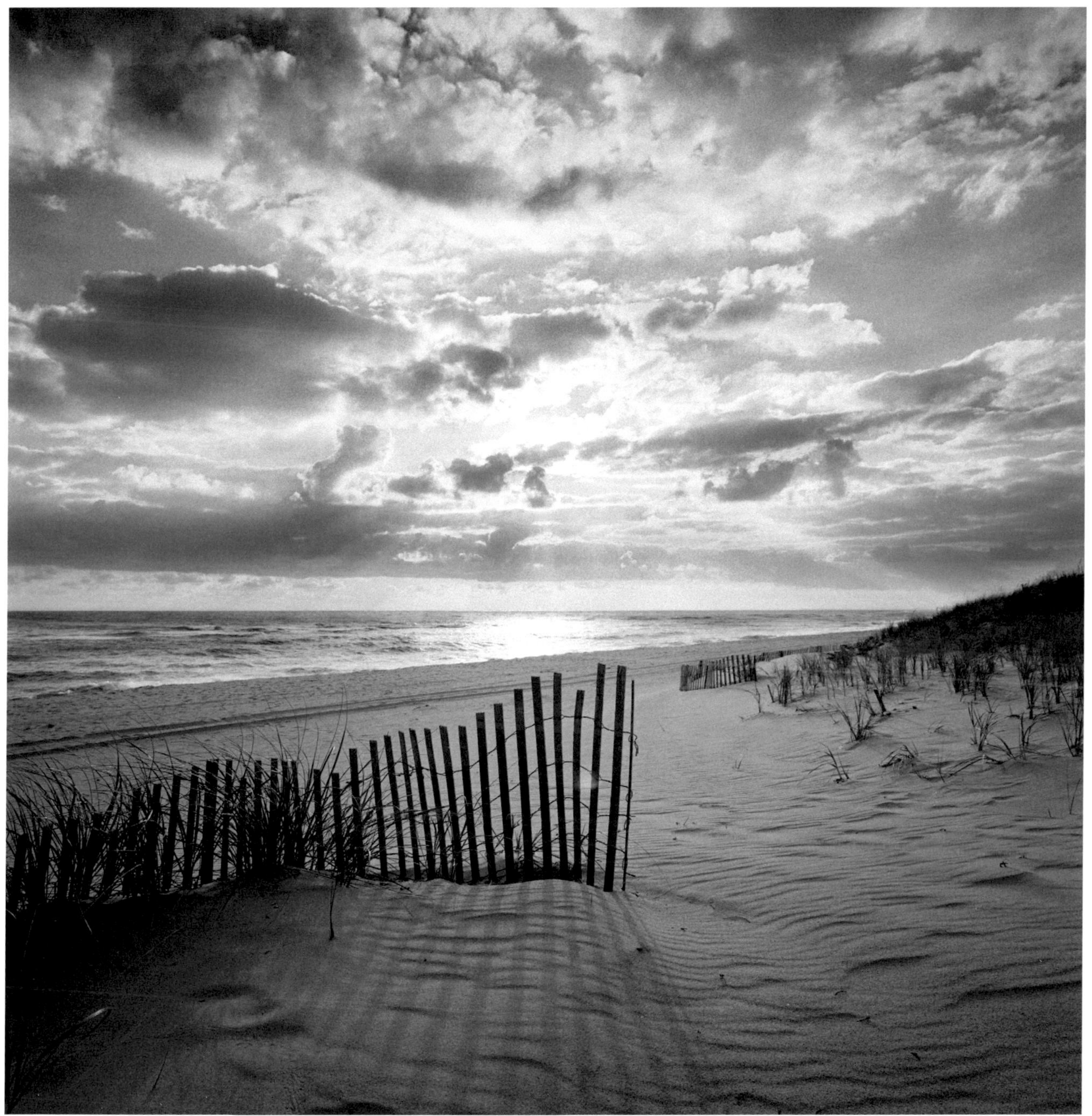

South Beach, 2006

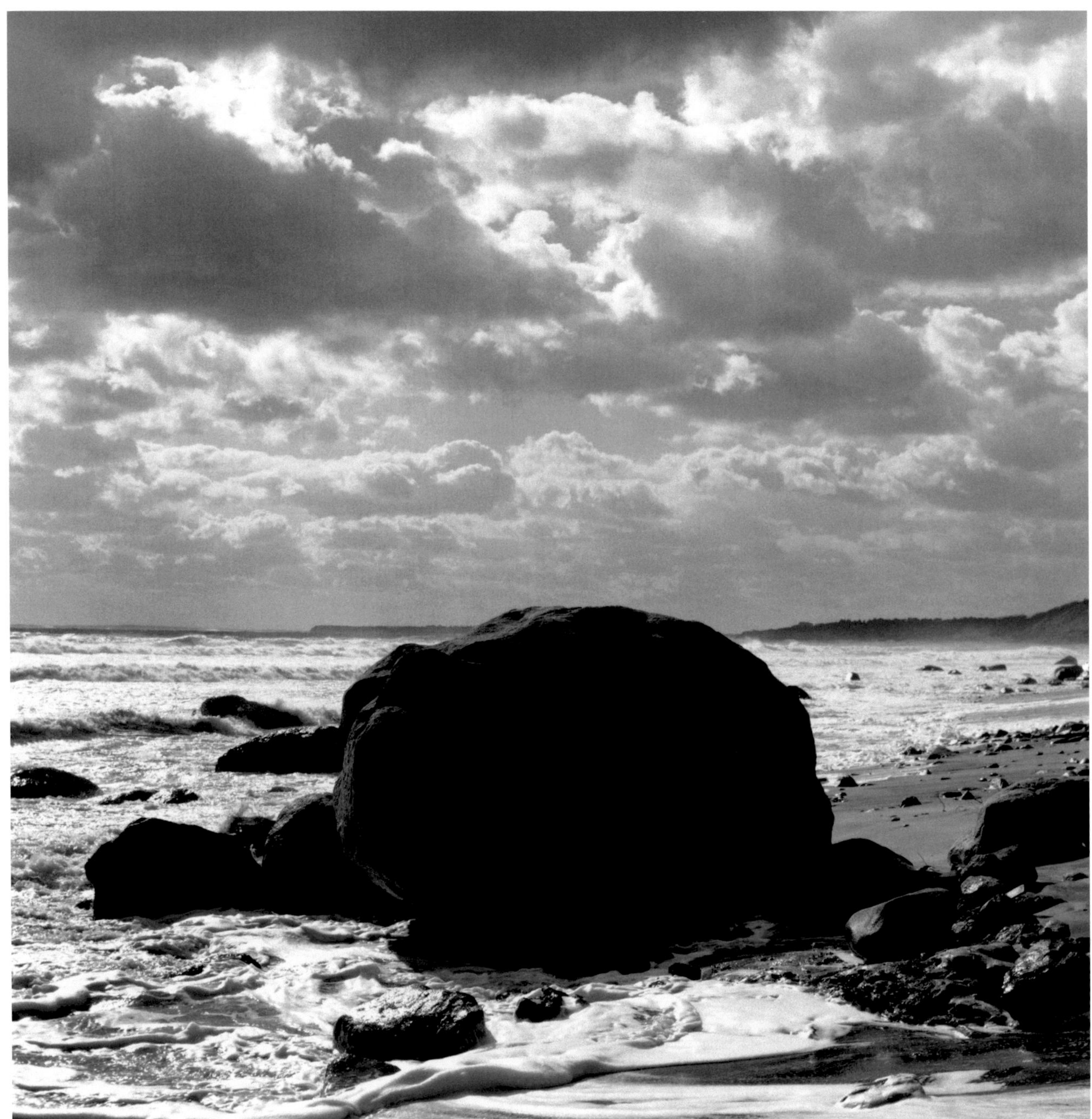

Lucy Vincent Beach, 2006

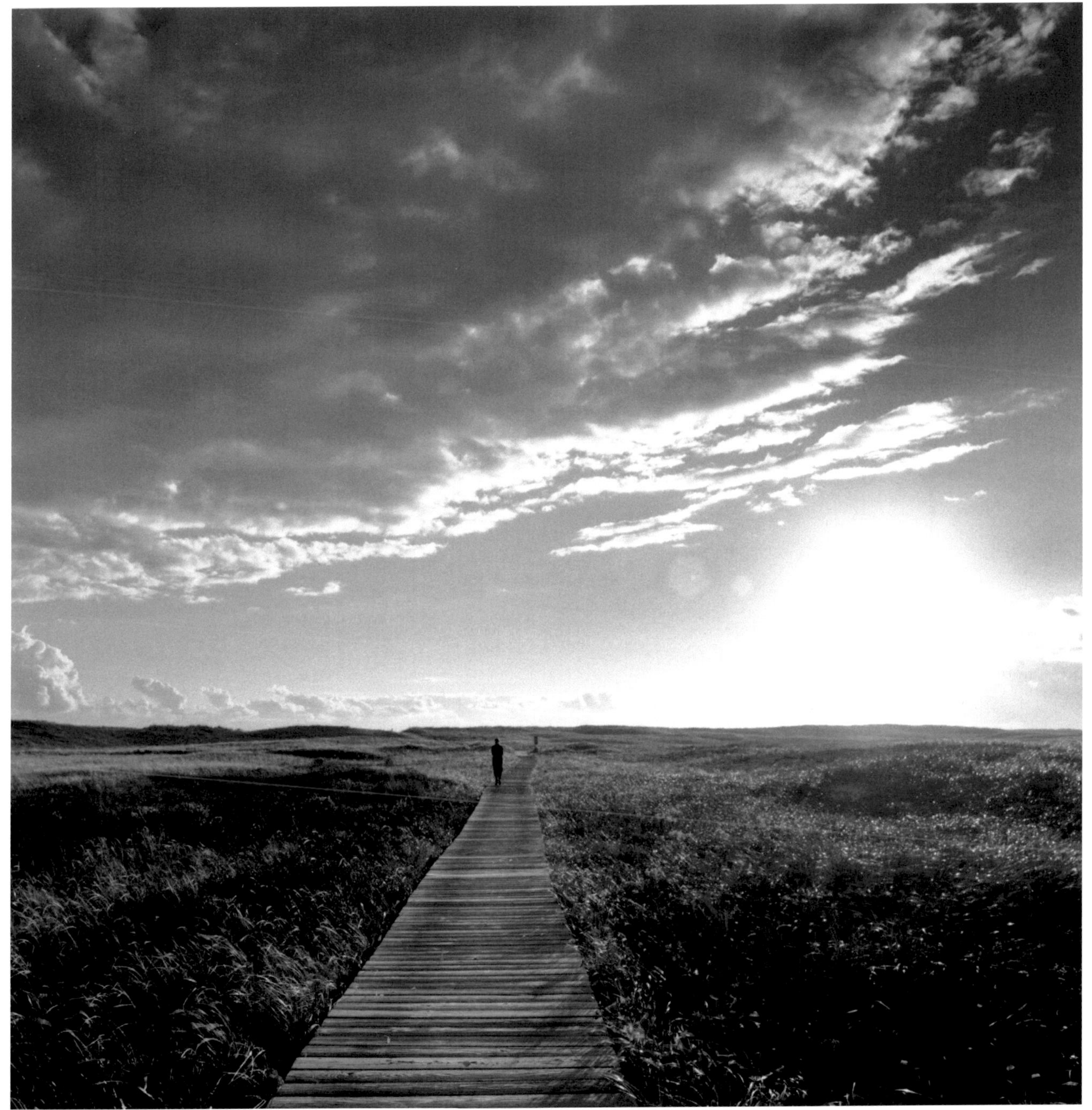

Wasque Point, 1999

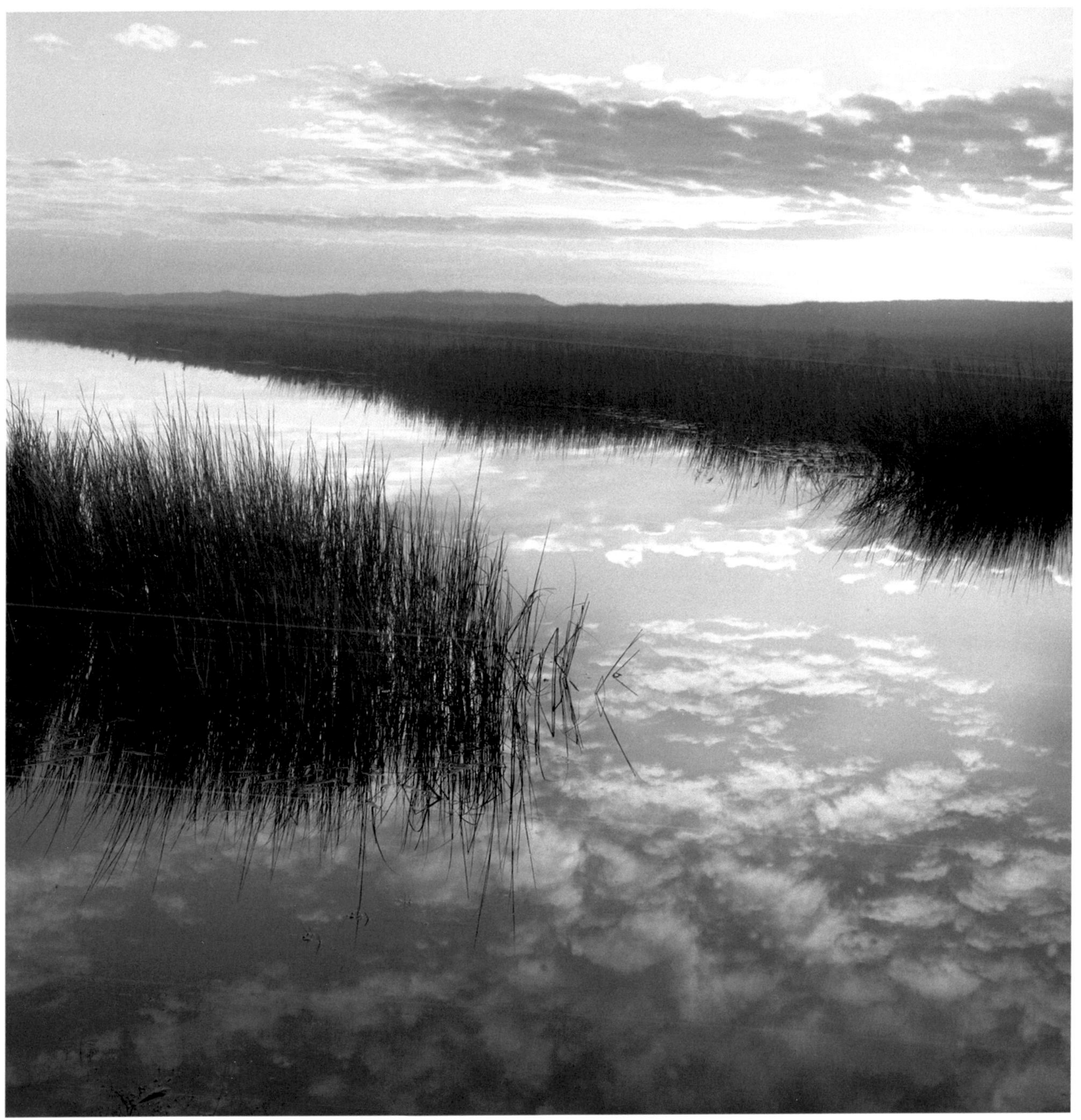

Tisbury Great Pond, 2000

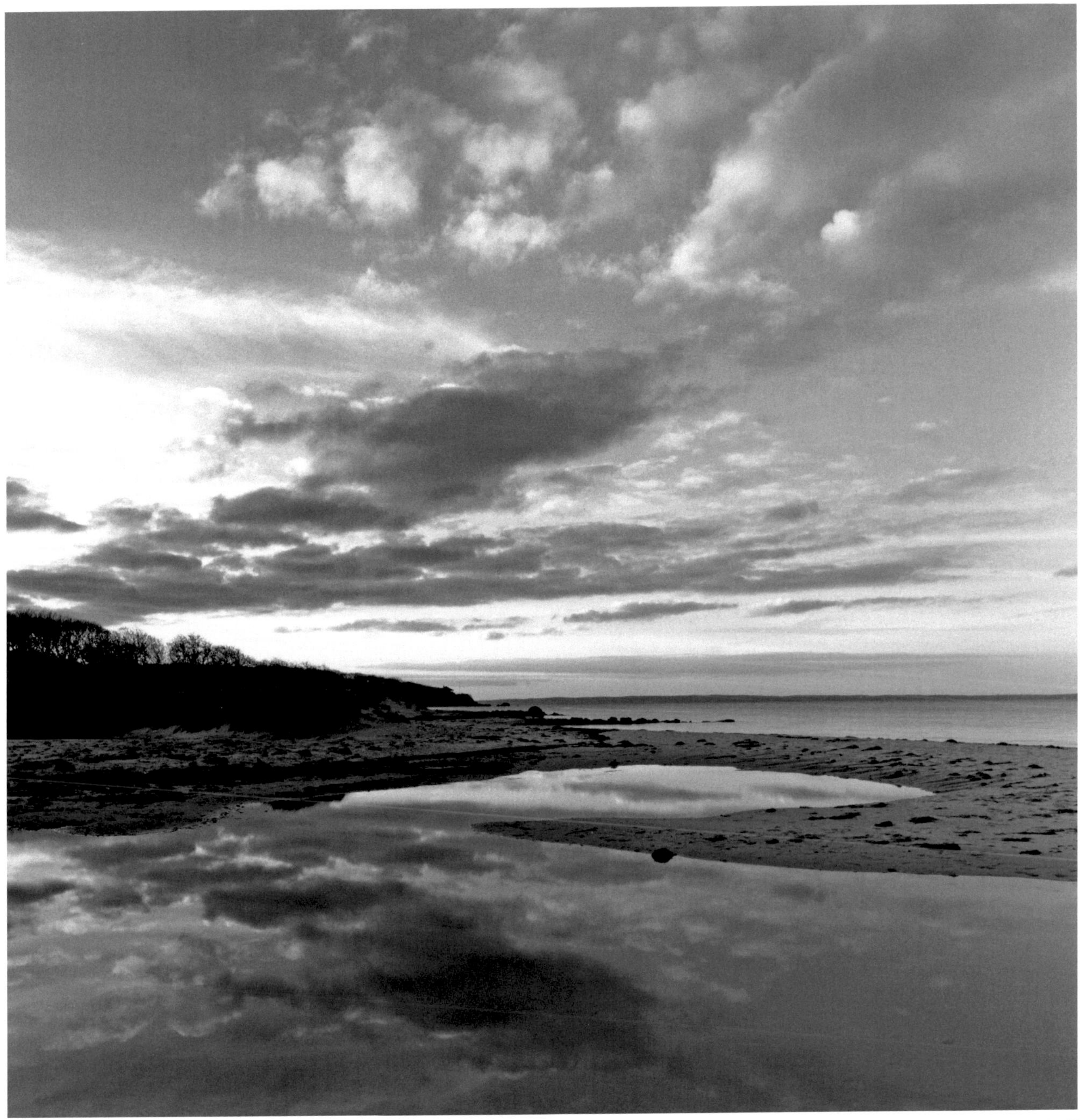

Lambert's Cove, 2012

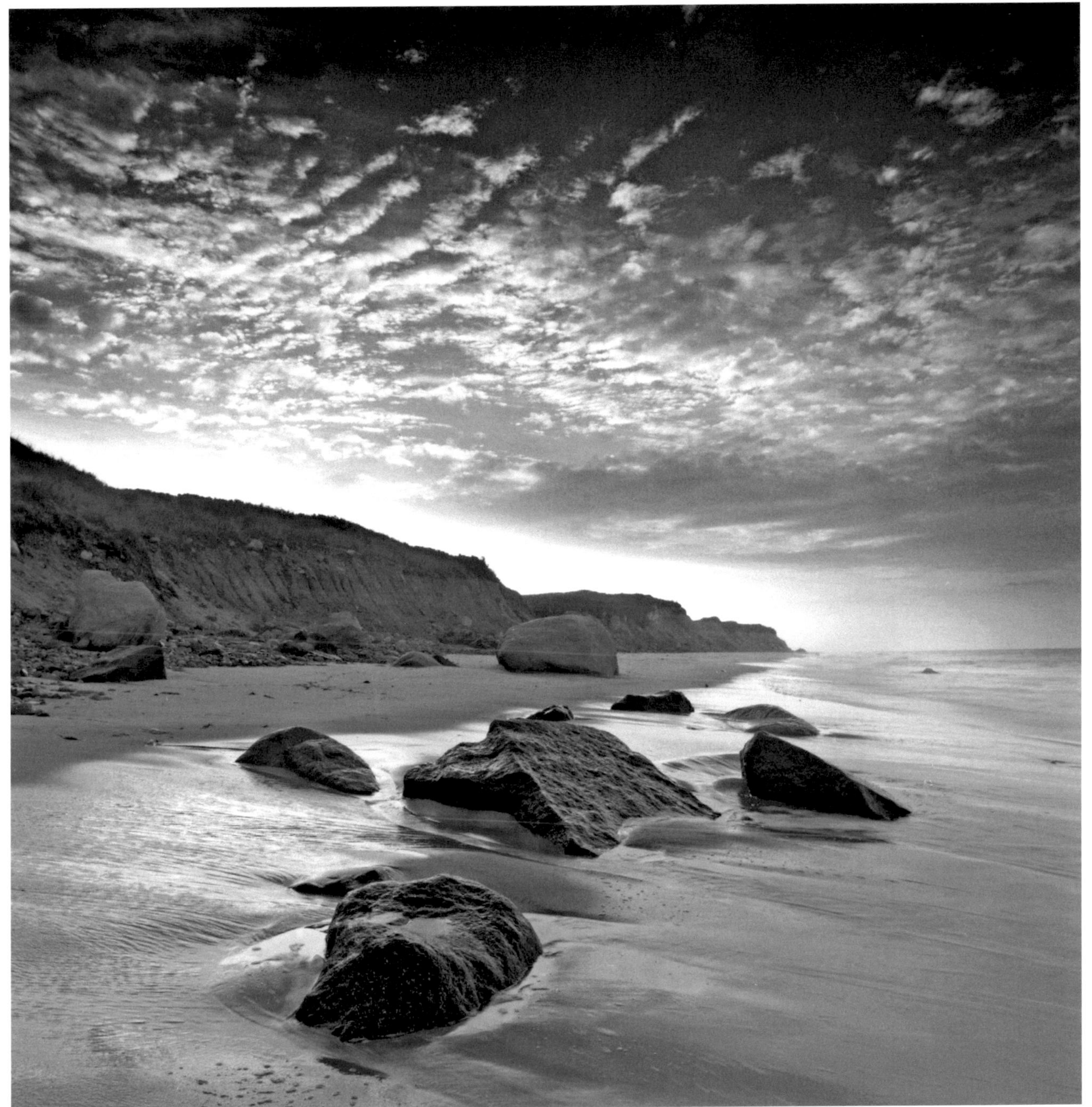

Zack's Cliffs, 2015

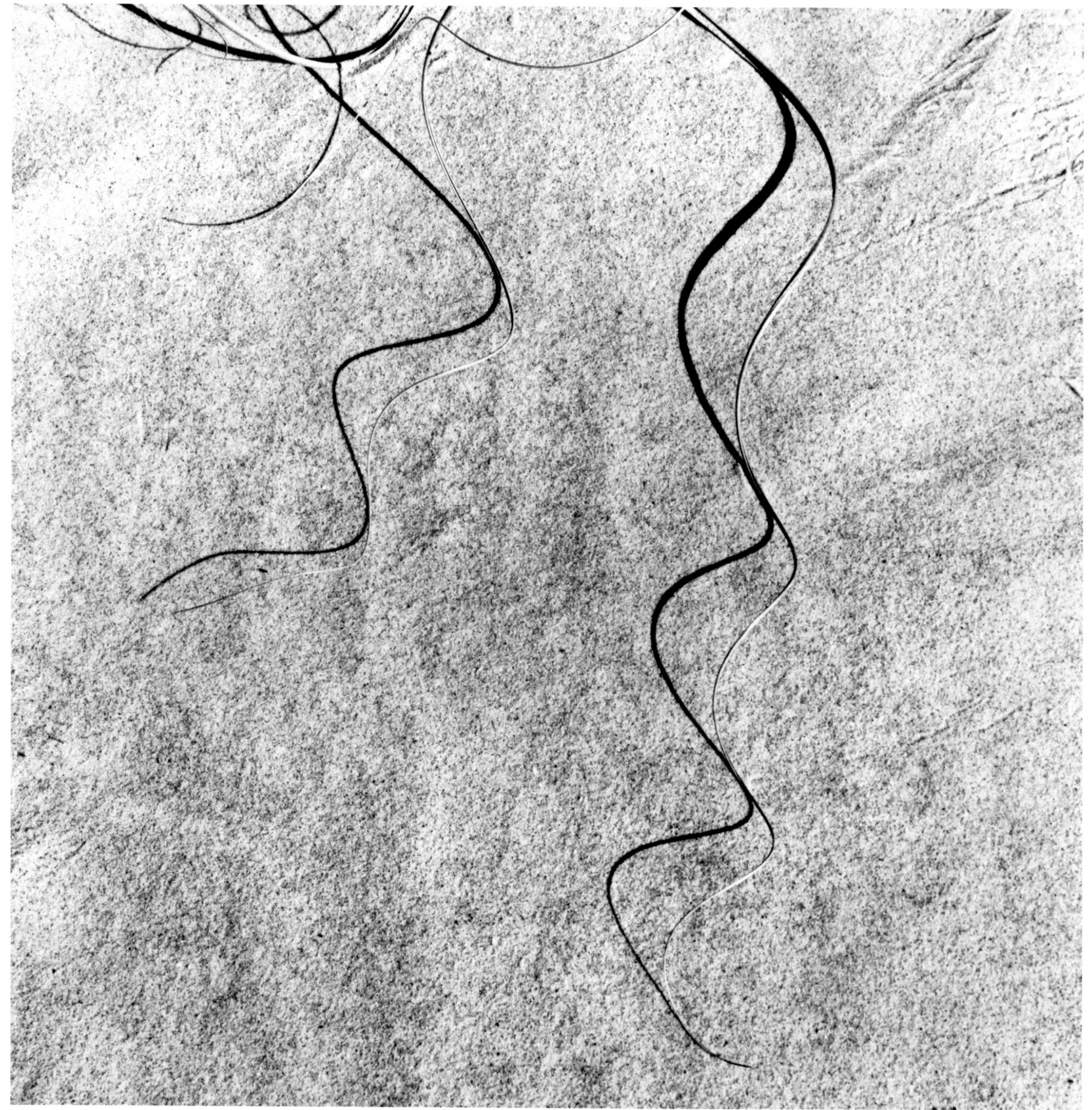

Stonewall Beach, 2012

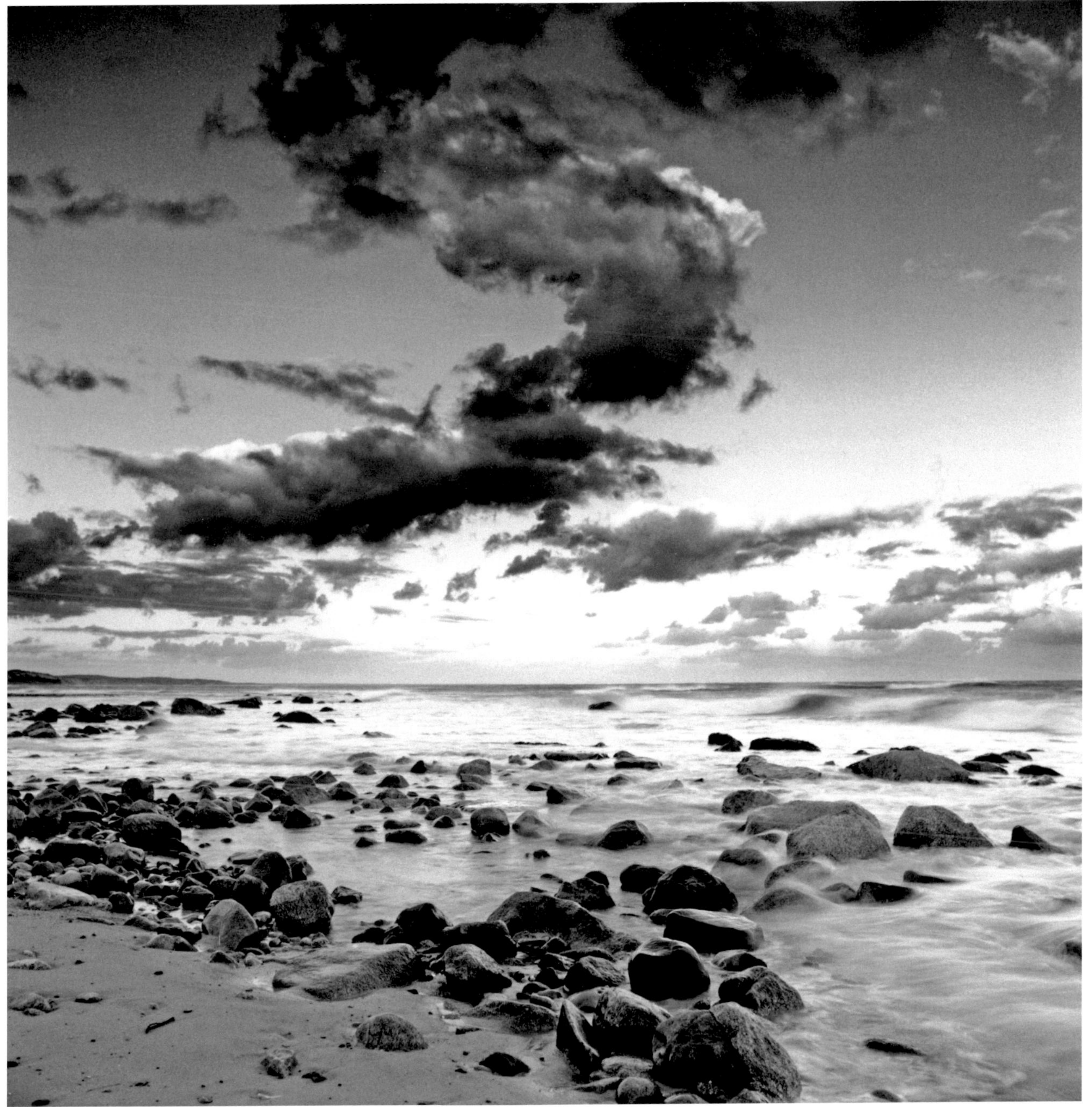

Squibnocket, 2001

HOW IT IS

PETER EVERWINE

This is how it is—

One turns away
and walks out into the evening.
There is a white horse on the prairie, or a river
that slips away among dark rocks.

One speaks, or is about to speak,
not that it matters.

What matters is this—

It is evening.
I have been away a long time.
Something is singing in the grass.

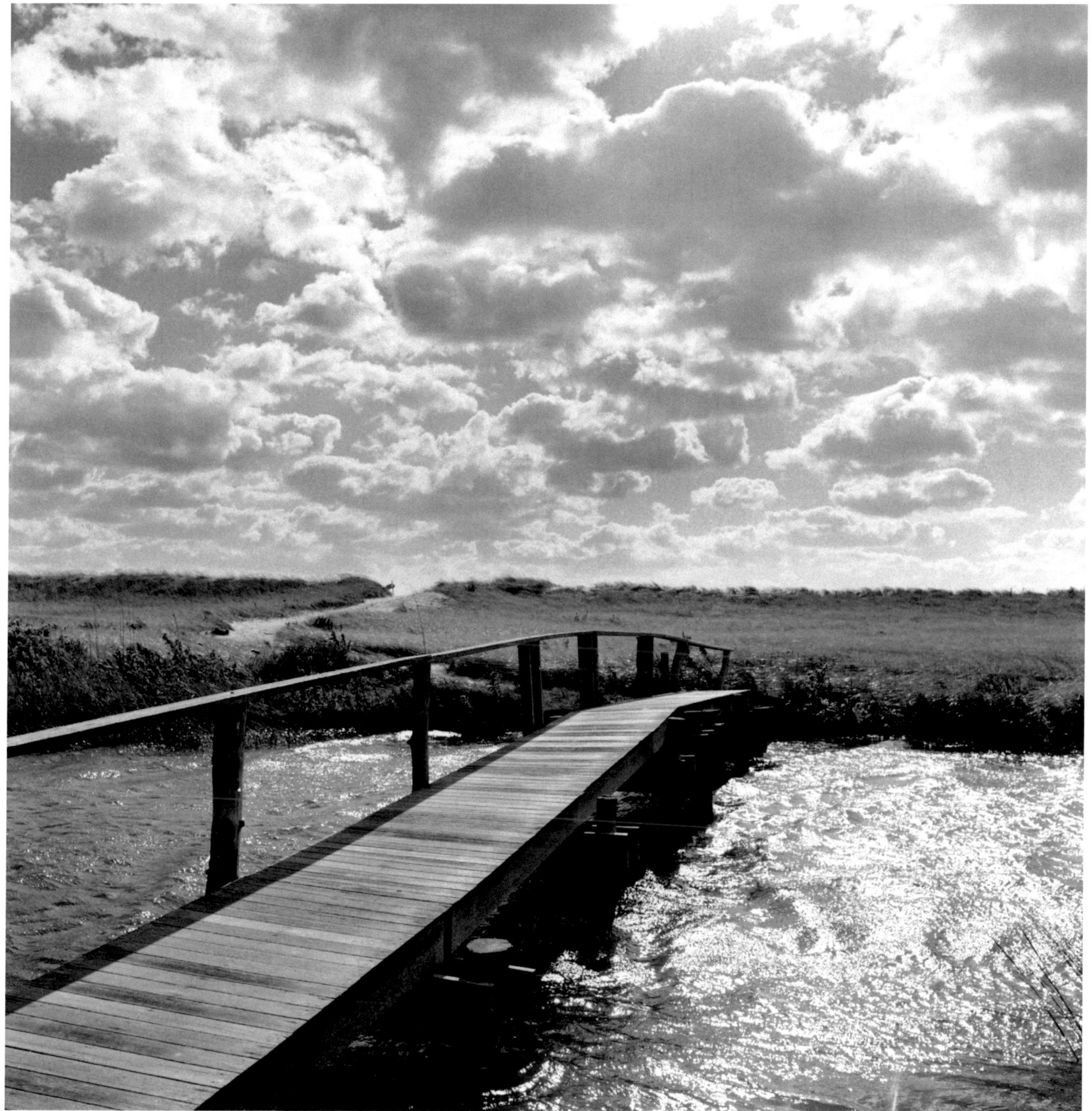

Quansoo, 2006

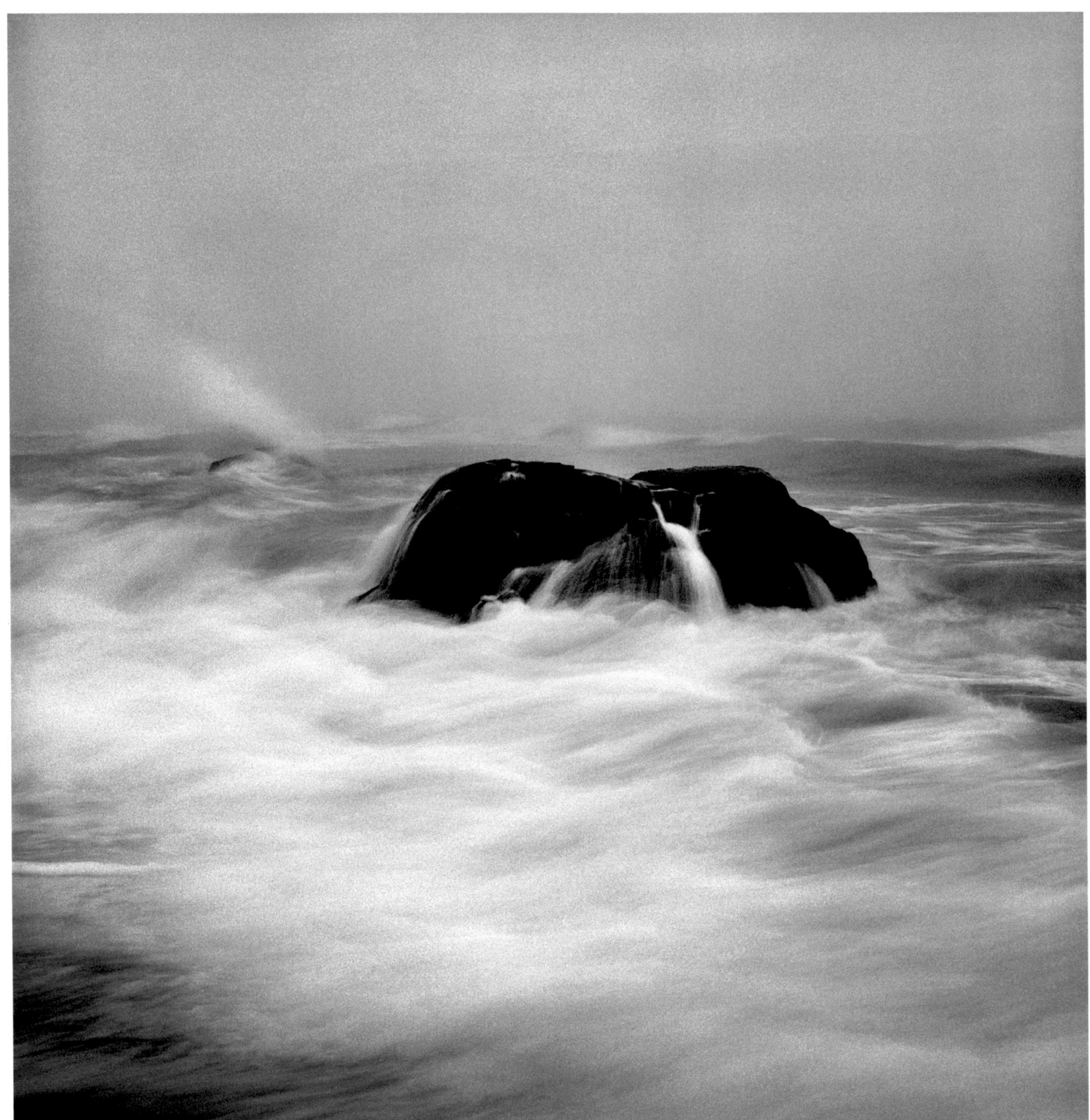

Lucy Vincent, 2004

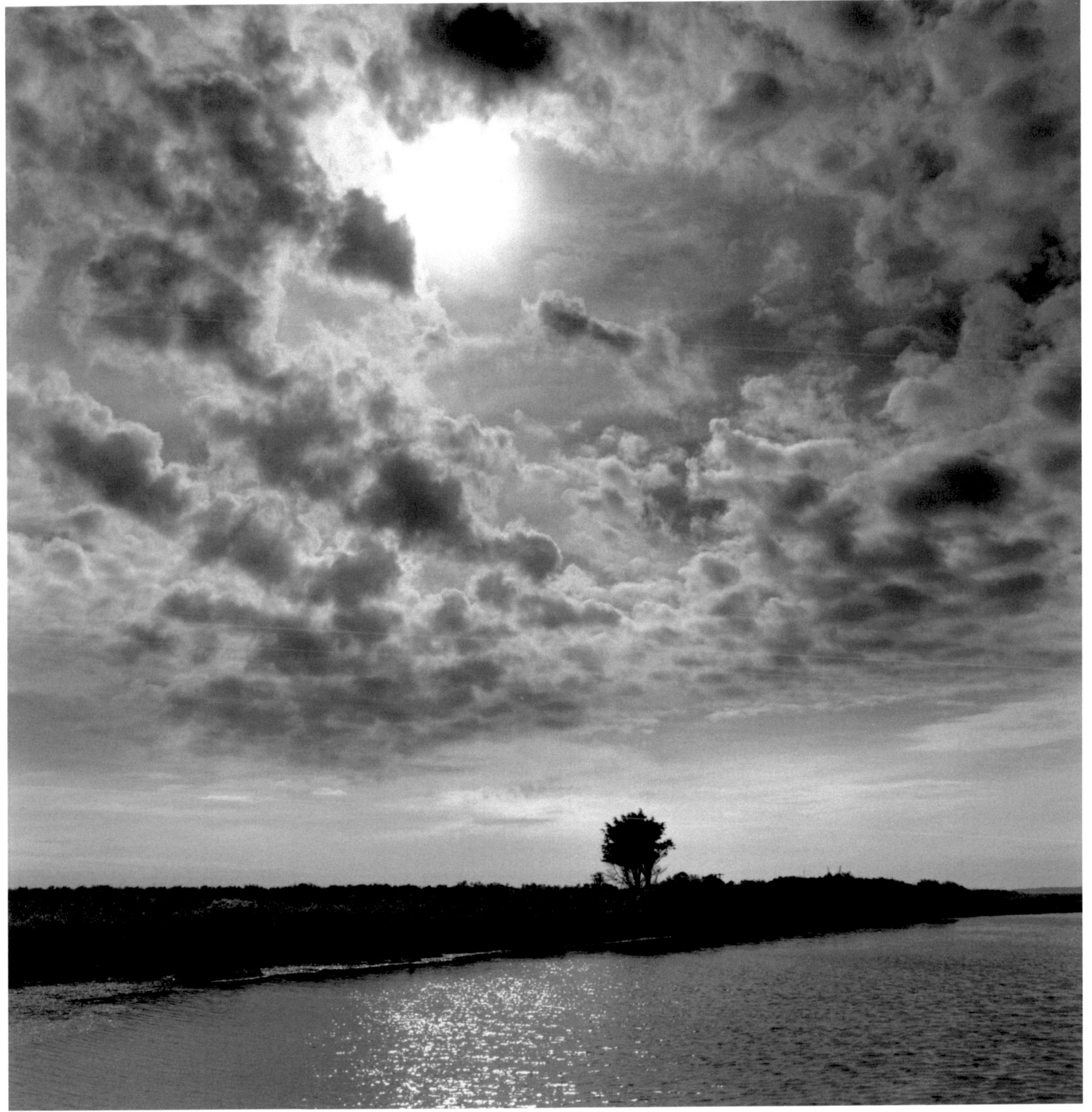

Long Point, 2012

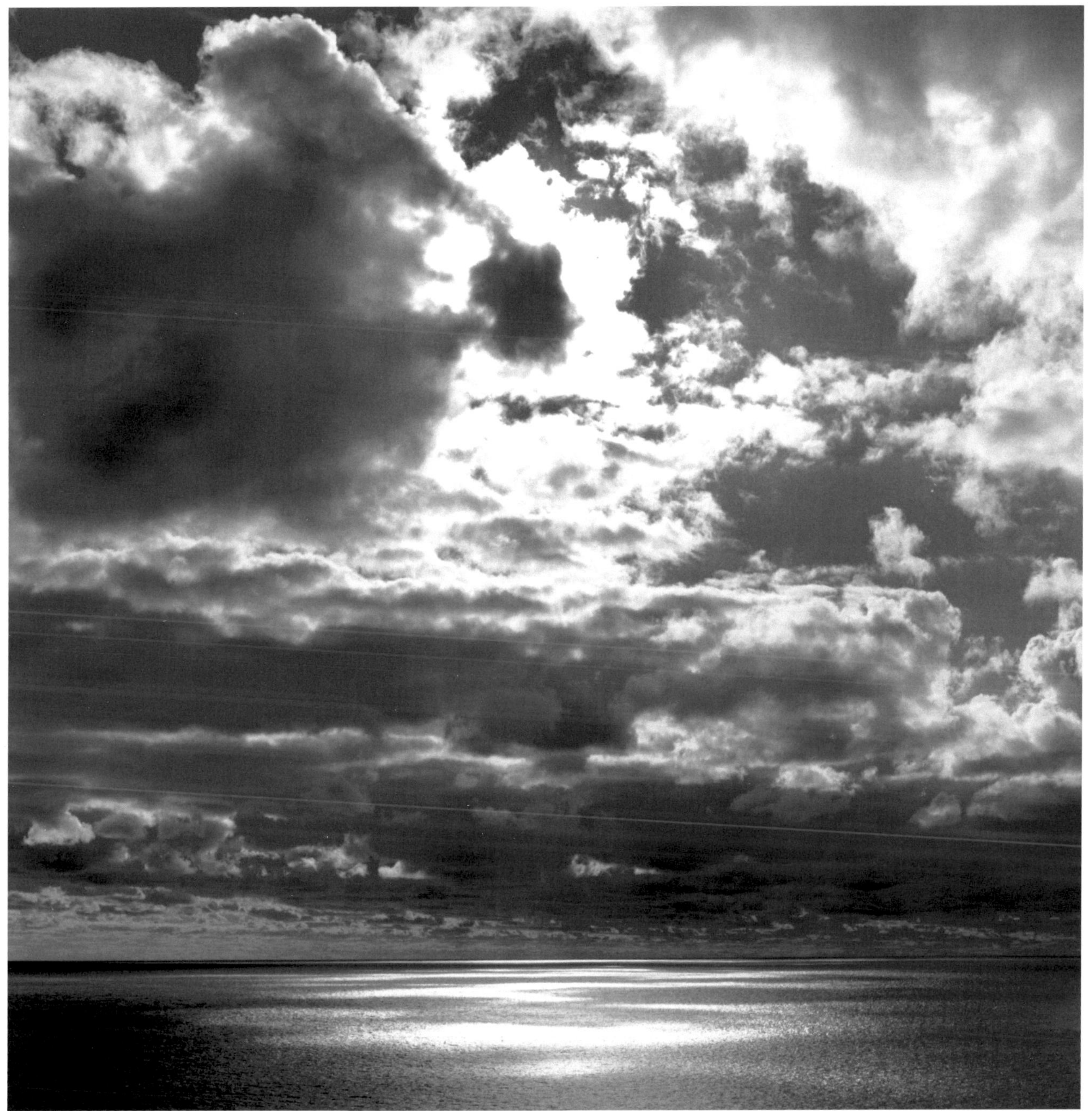

Aquinnah, 2001

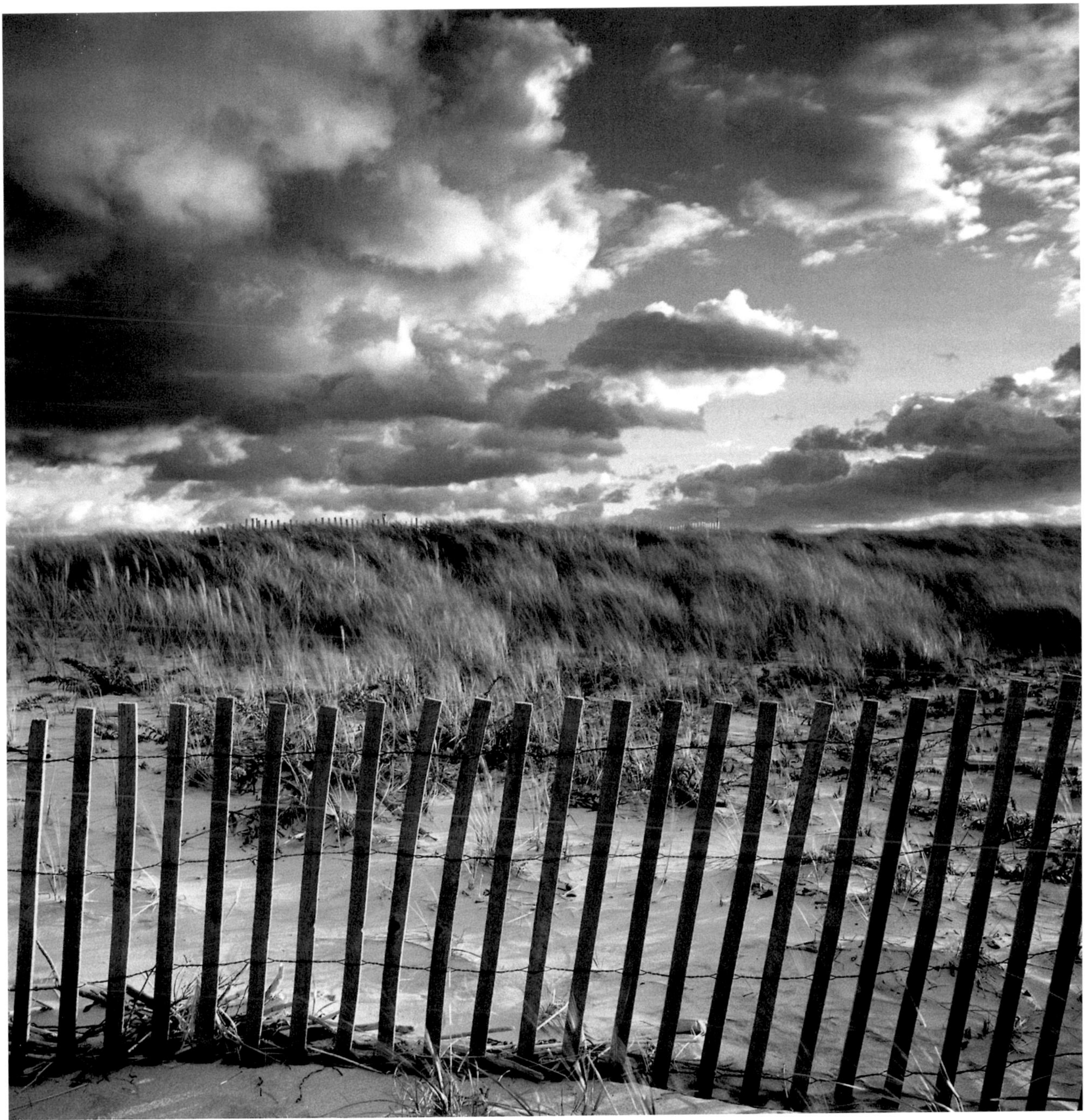

Chilmark Pond, 1999

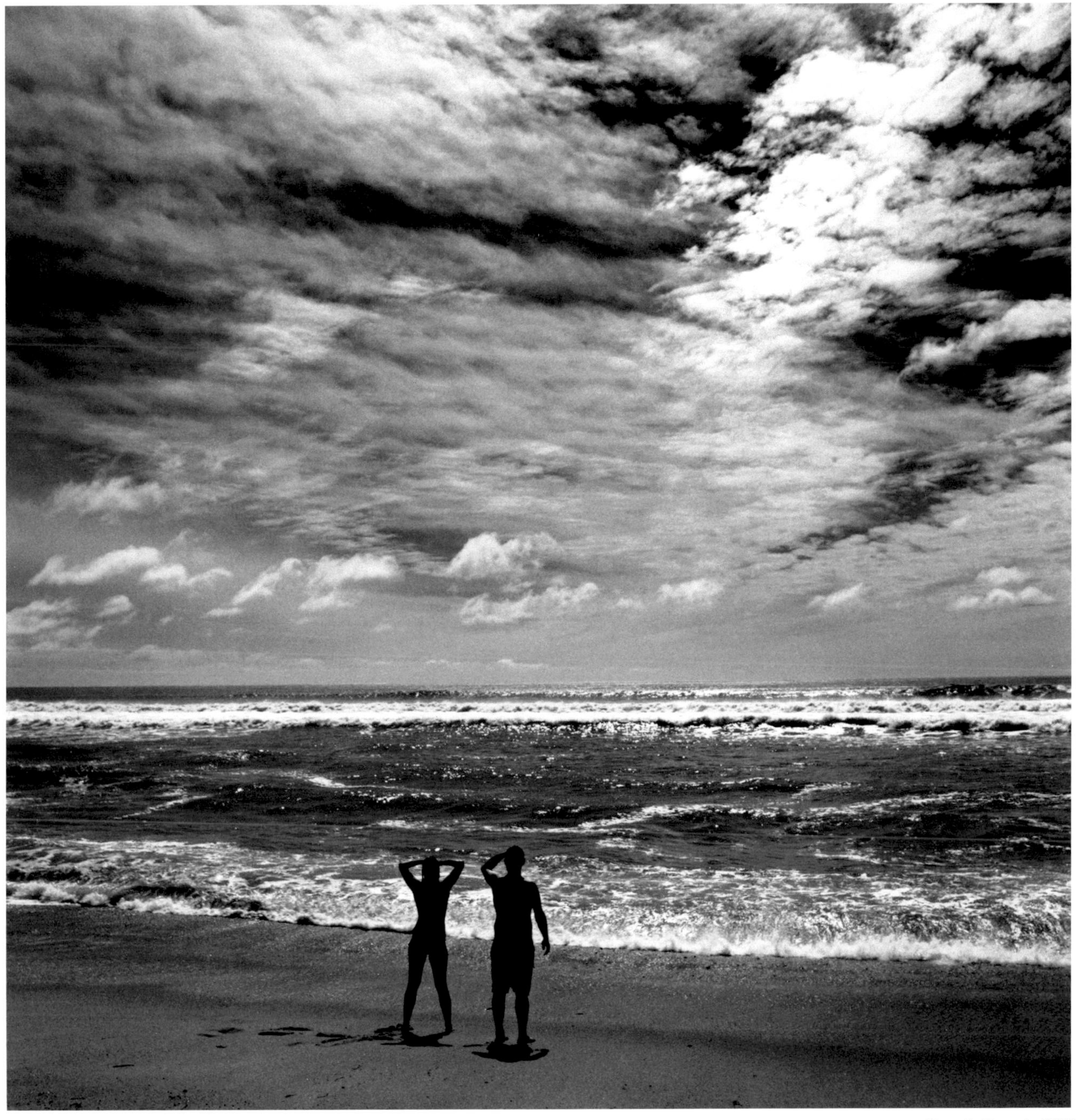

South Beach, 2011

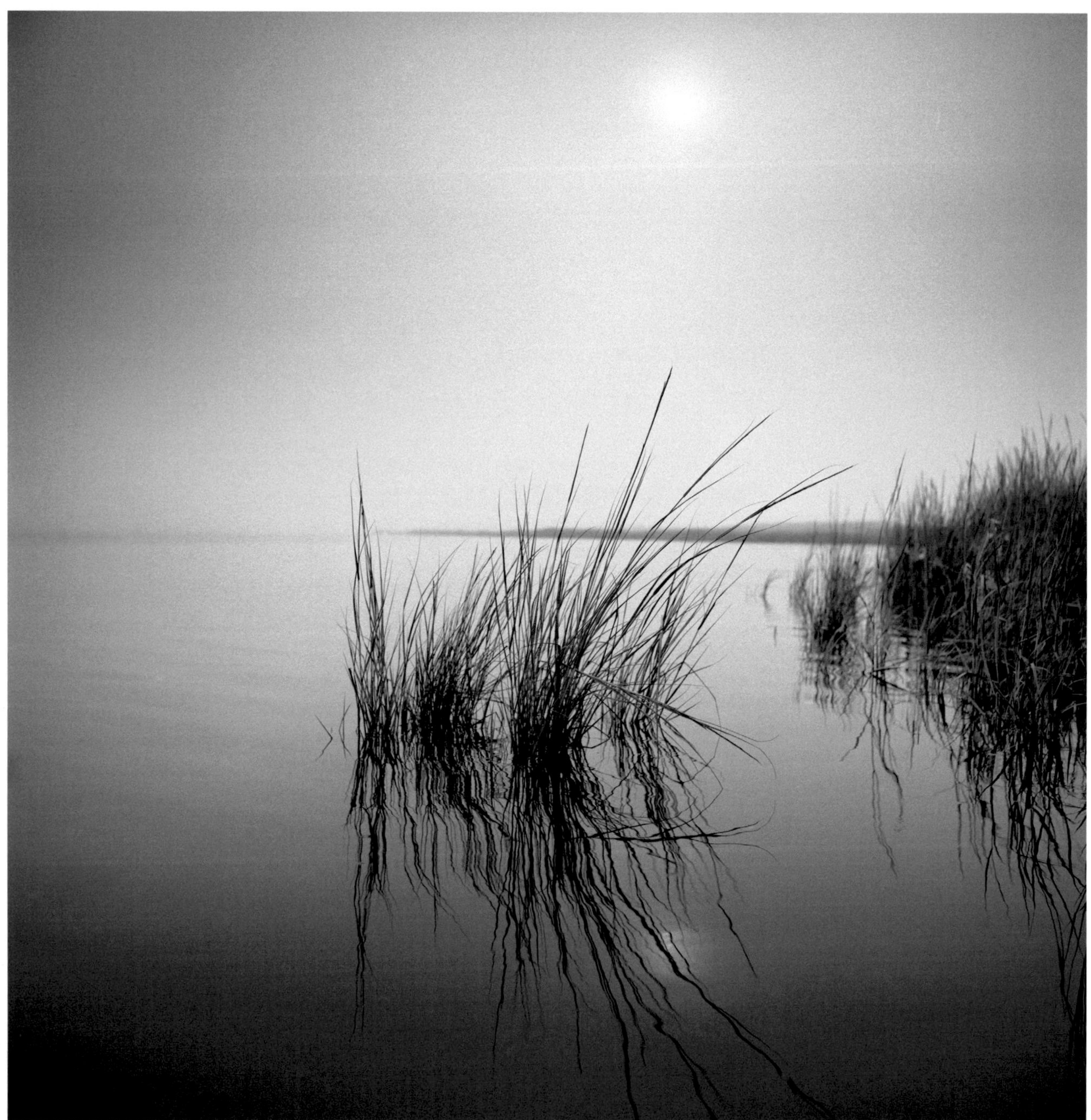

Herring Creek, 2011

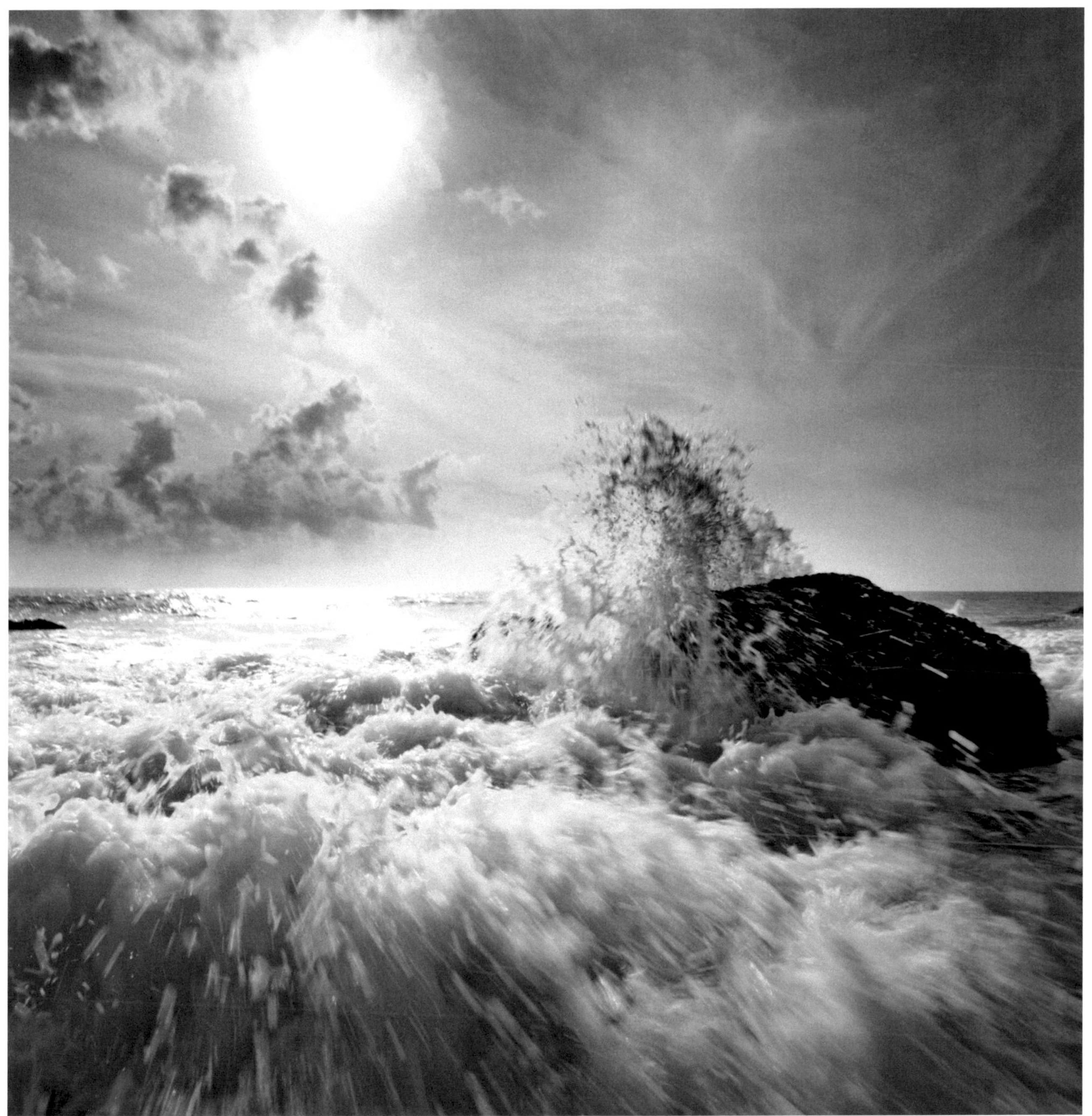

Philbin Beach, 2015

THE SUN

CZESŁAW MIŁOSZ

All colors come from the sun. And it does not have
Any particular color, for it contains them all.
And the whole Earth is like a poem
While the sun above represents the artist.

Whoever wants to paint the variegated world
Let him never look straight up at the sun
Or he will lose the memory of things he has seen.
Only burning tears will stay in his eyes.

Let him kneel down, lower his face to the grass,
And look at the light reflected by the ground.
There he will find everything we have lost:
The stars and the roses, the dusks and the dawns.

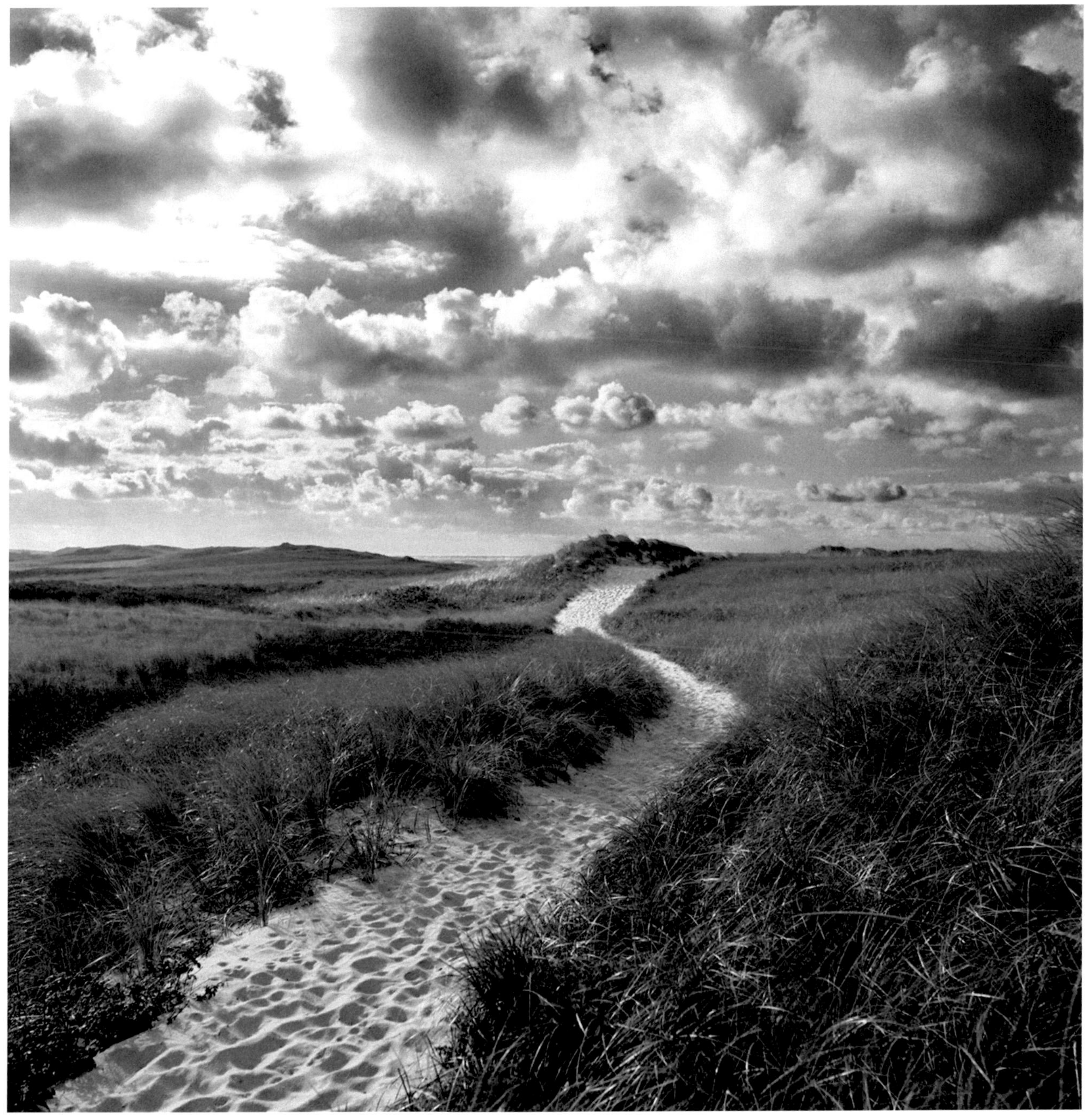

Philbin Beach, 1999

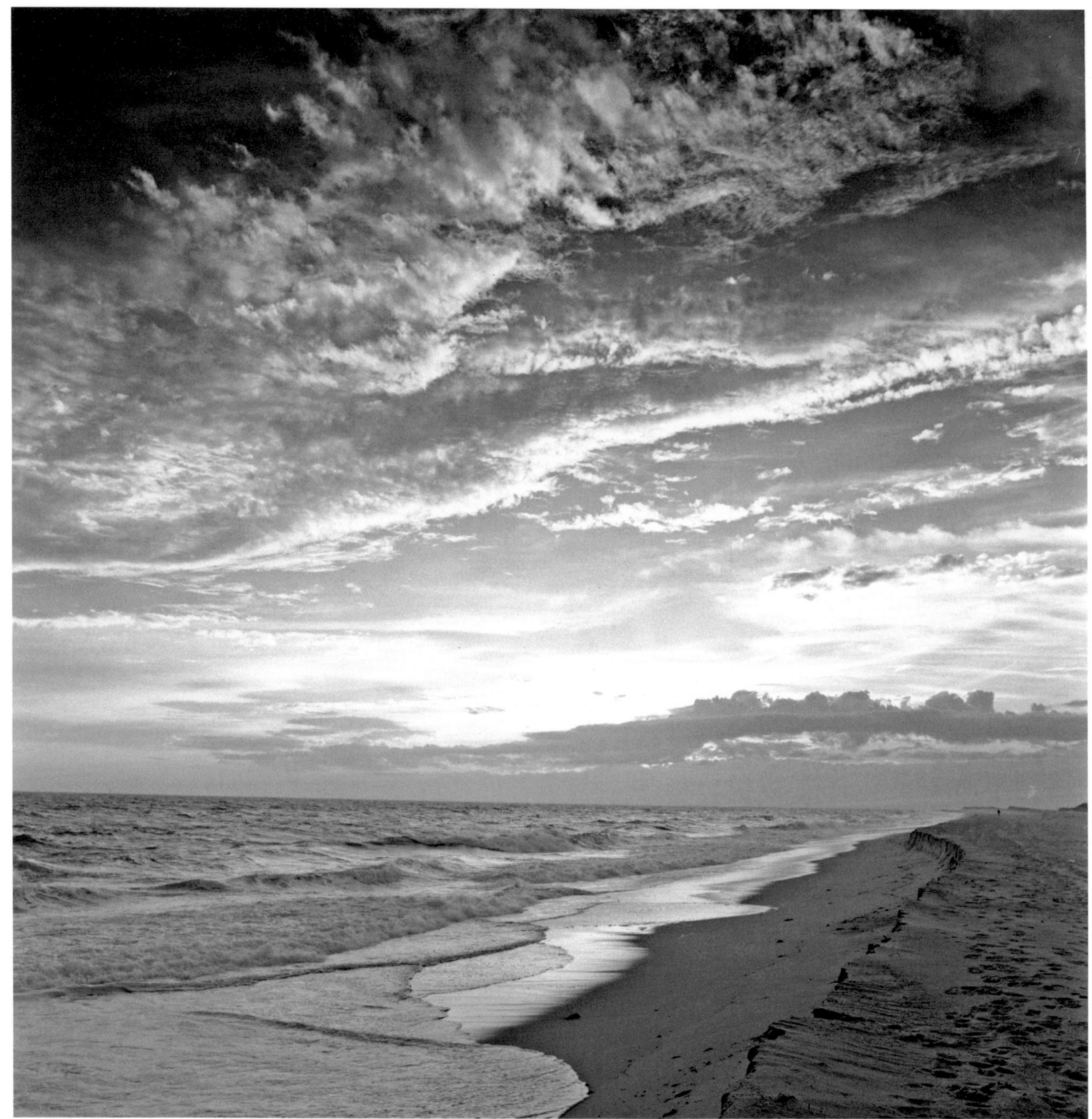

South Shore, 2012

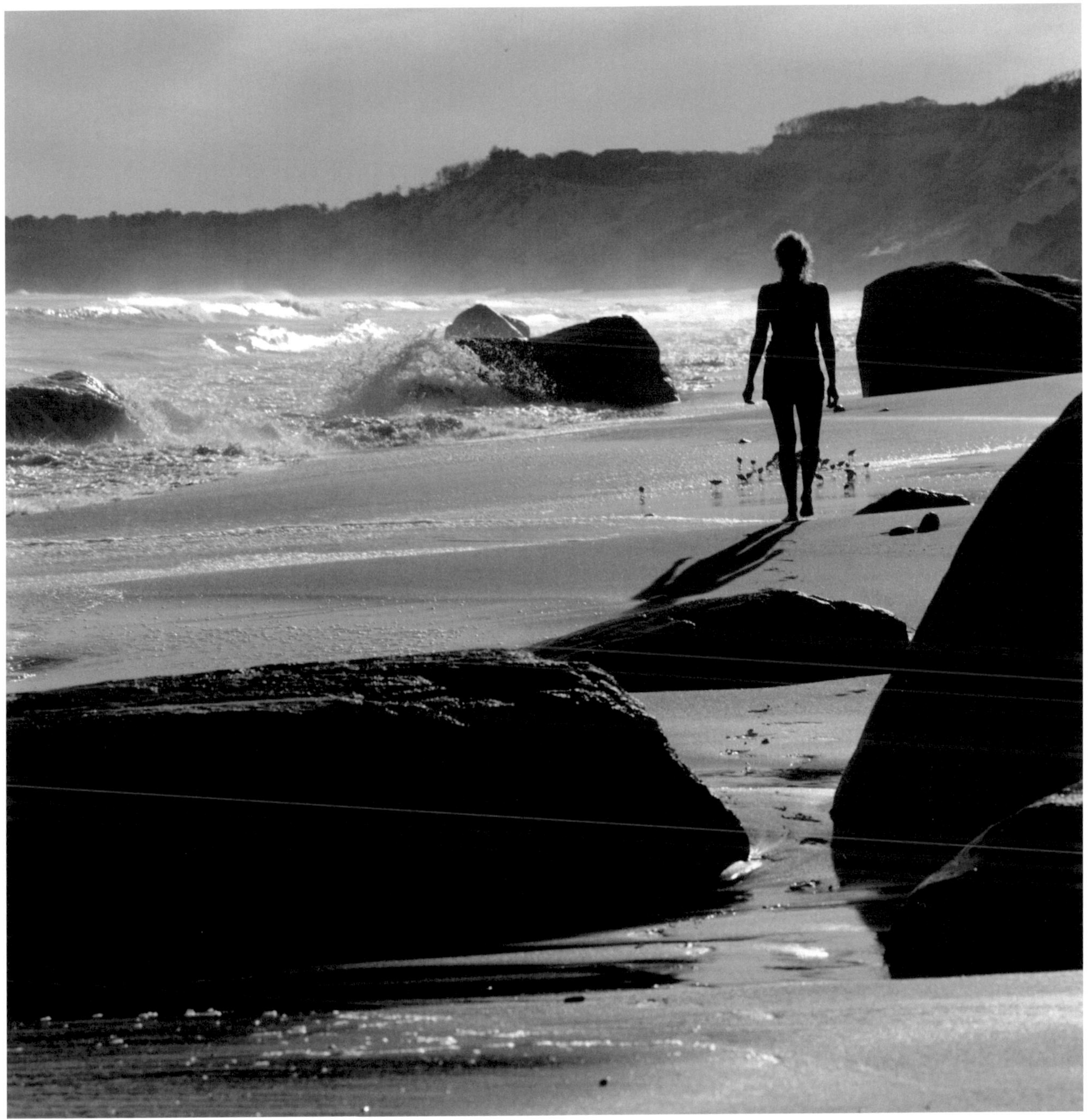

Wequobsque Cliffs, 2011

Blackpoint Pond, 2016

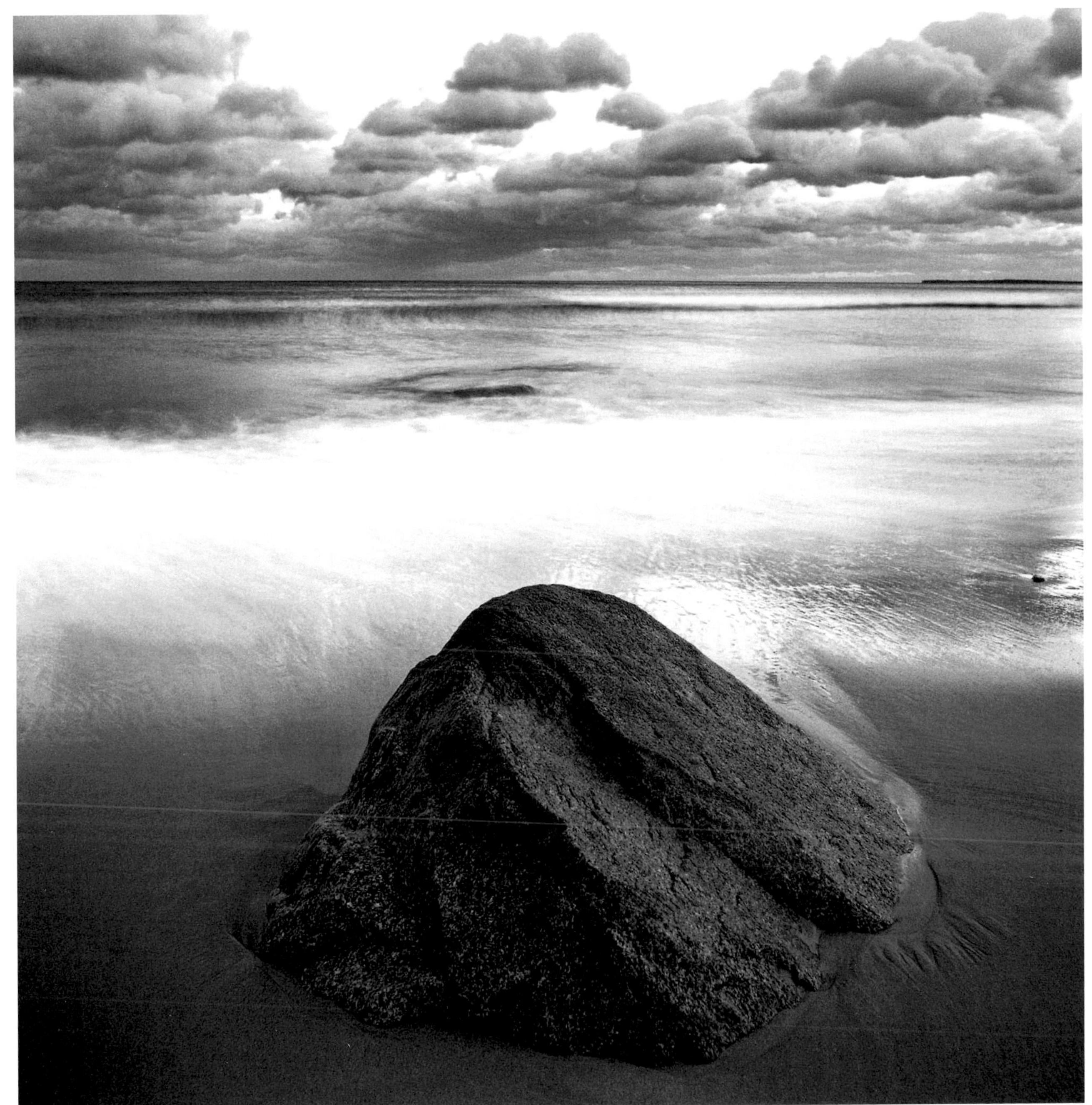

Squibnocket Point, 1999

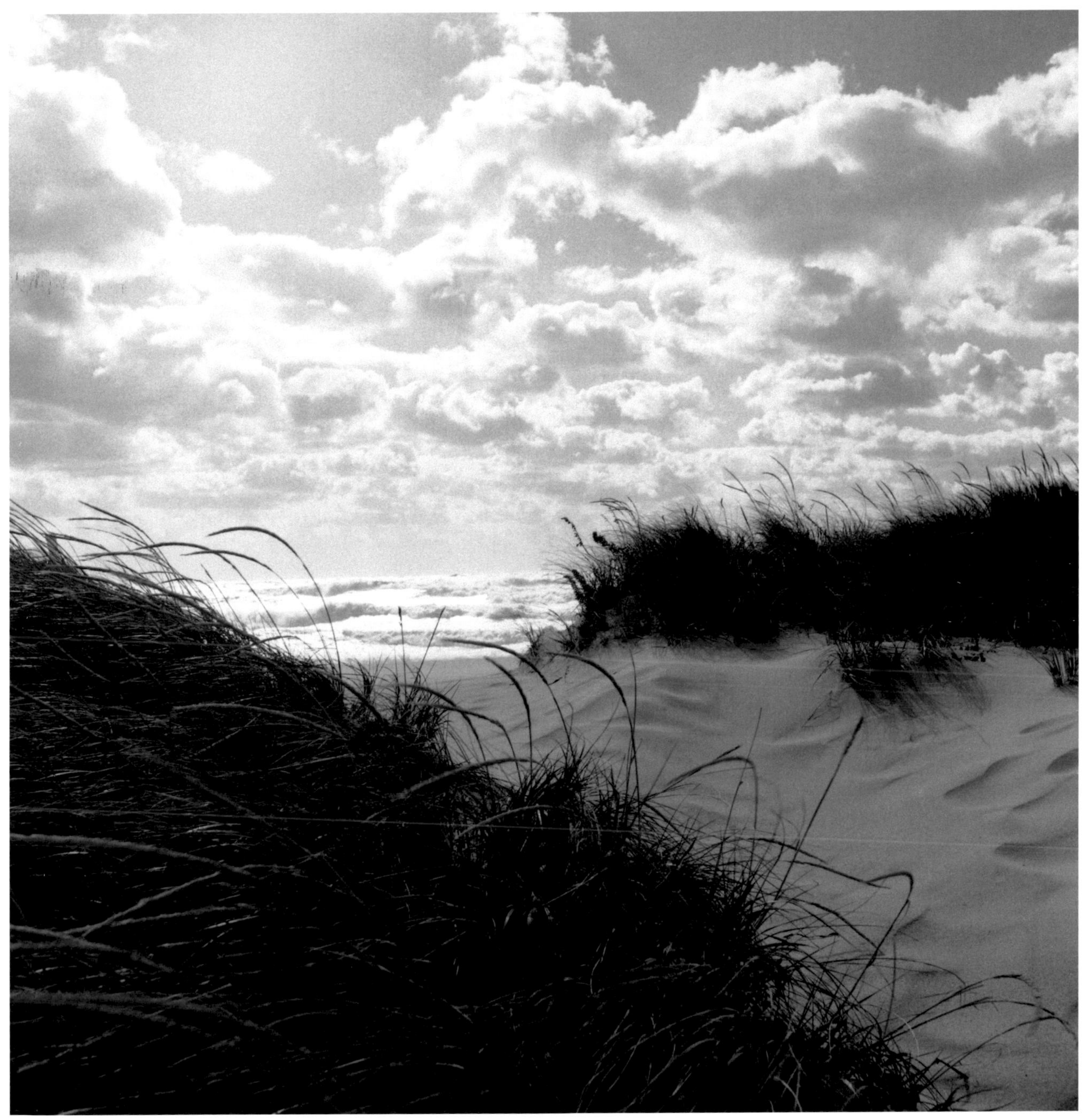

Norton Point Beach, 2006

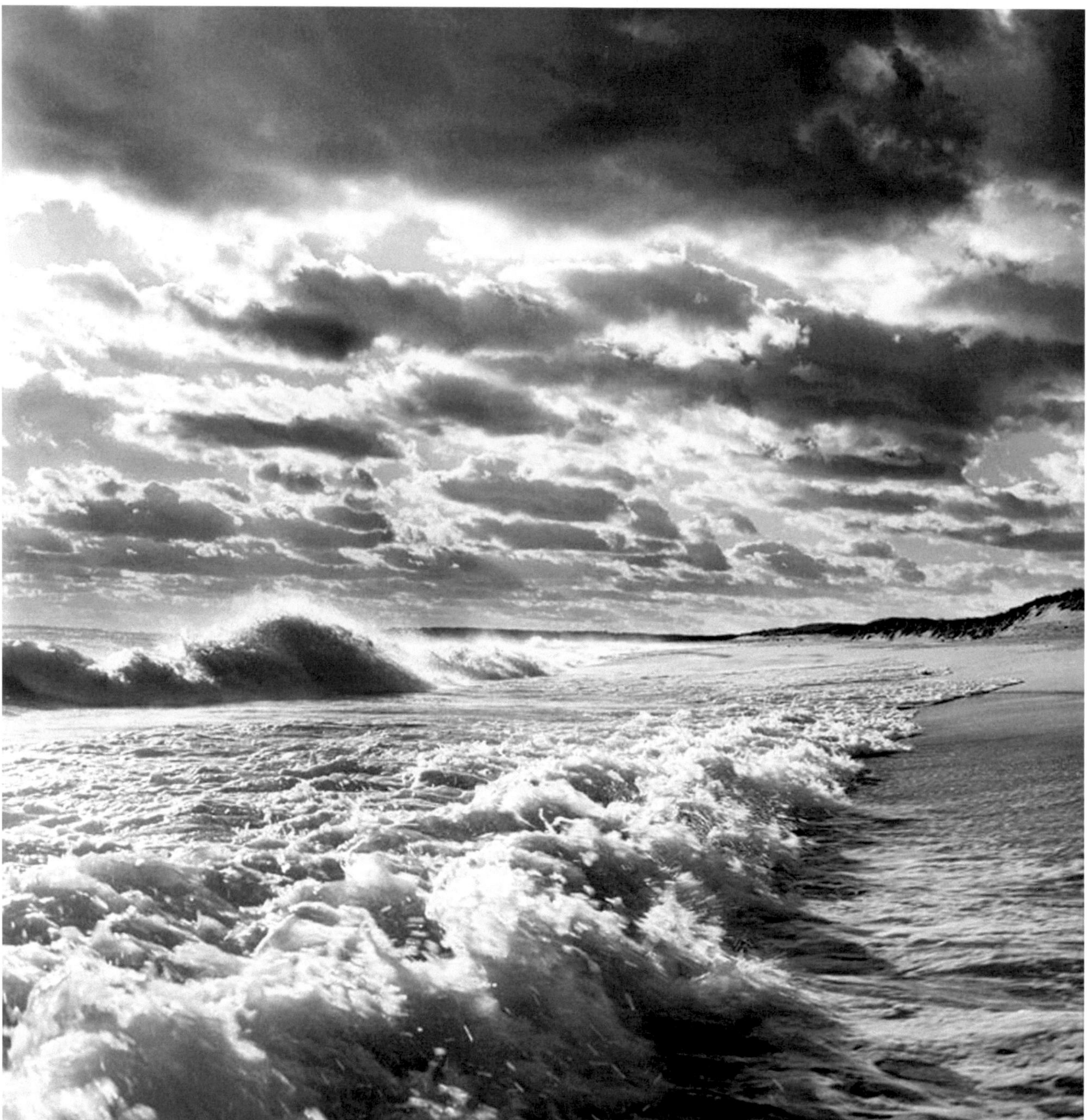

Tisbury Great Pond Beach, 2002

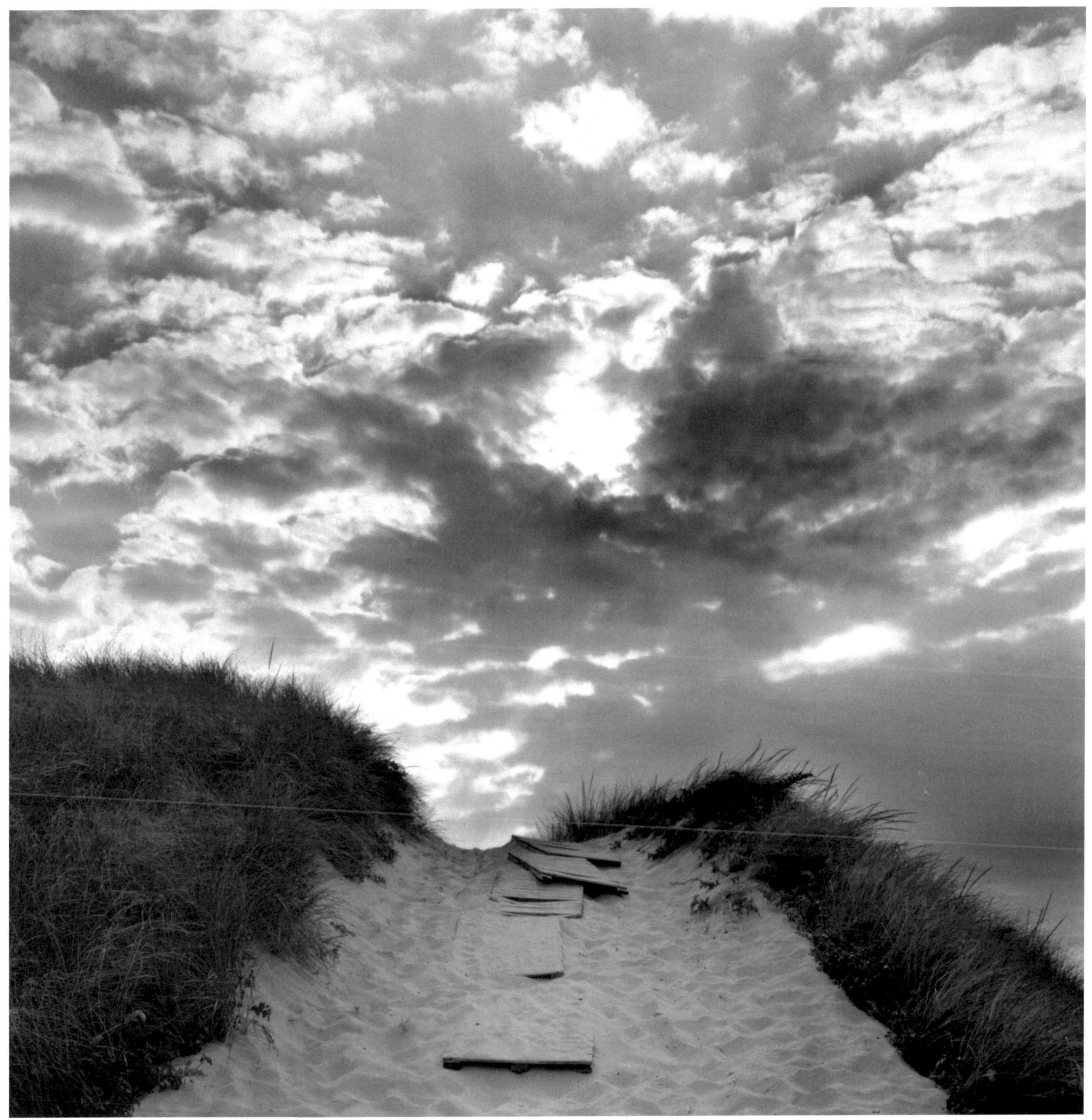

Philbin Beach, 1998

TO WHAT LISTENS

WENDELL BERRY

I come to it again
and again, the thought of the wren
opening his song here
to no human ear—
no woman to look up,
no man to turn his head.
The farm will sink then
from all we have done and said.
Beauty will lie, fold
on fold, upon it. Foreseeing
it so, I cannot withhold
love. But from the height
and distance of foresight,
how well I like it
as it is! The river shining,
the bare trees on the bank,
the house set snug
as a stone in the hill's flank,
the pasture behind it green.
Its songs and loves throb
in my head till like the wren
I sing—to what listens—again.

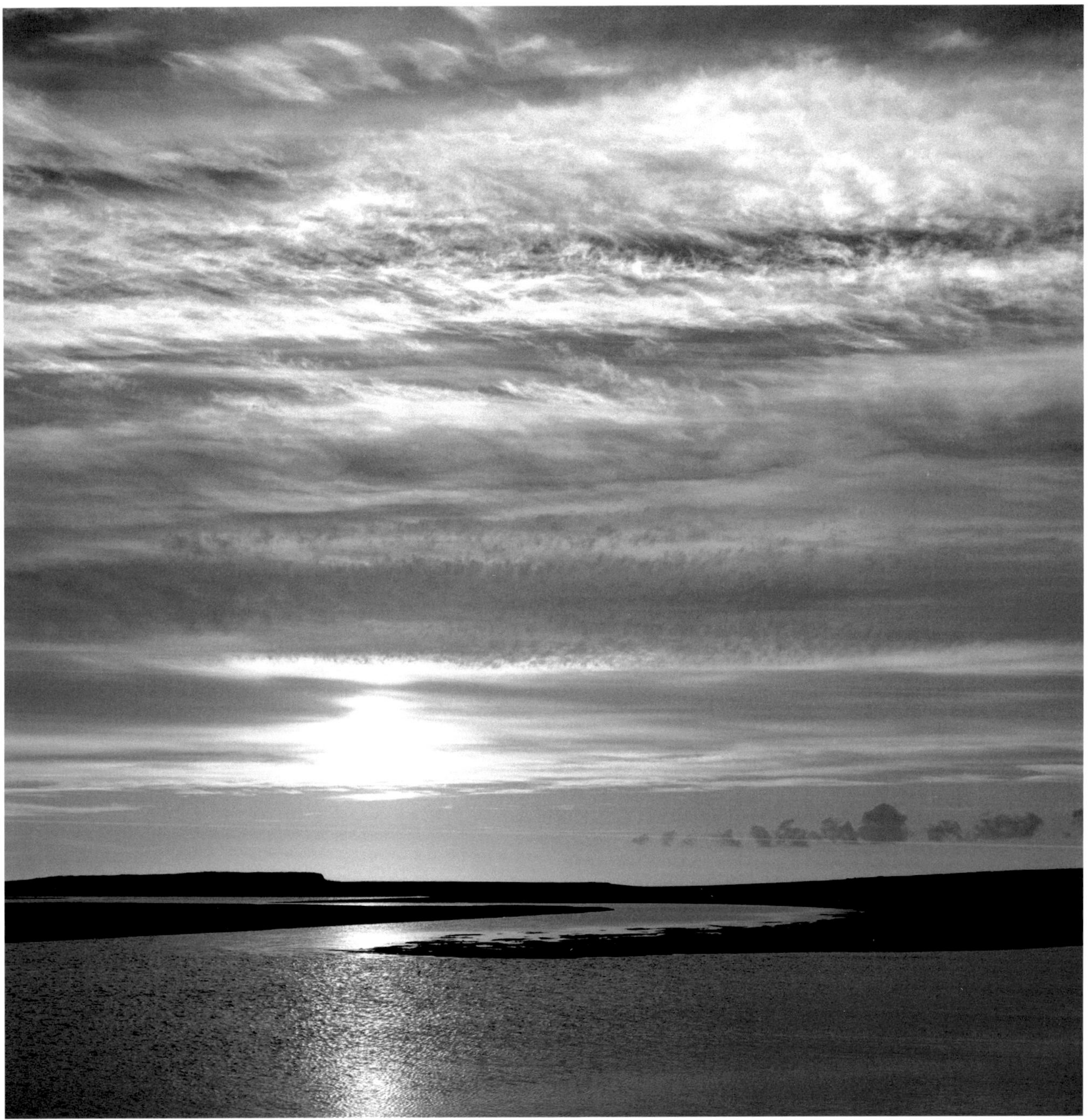

Tisbury Great Pond Beach, 2001

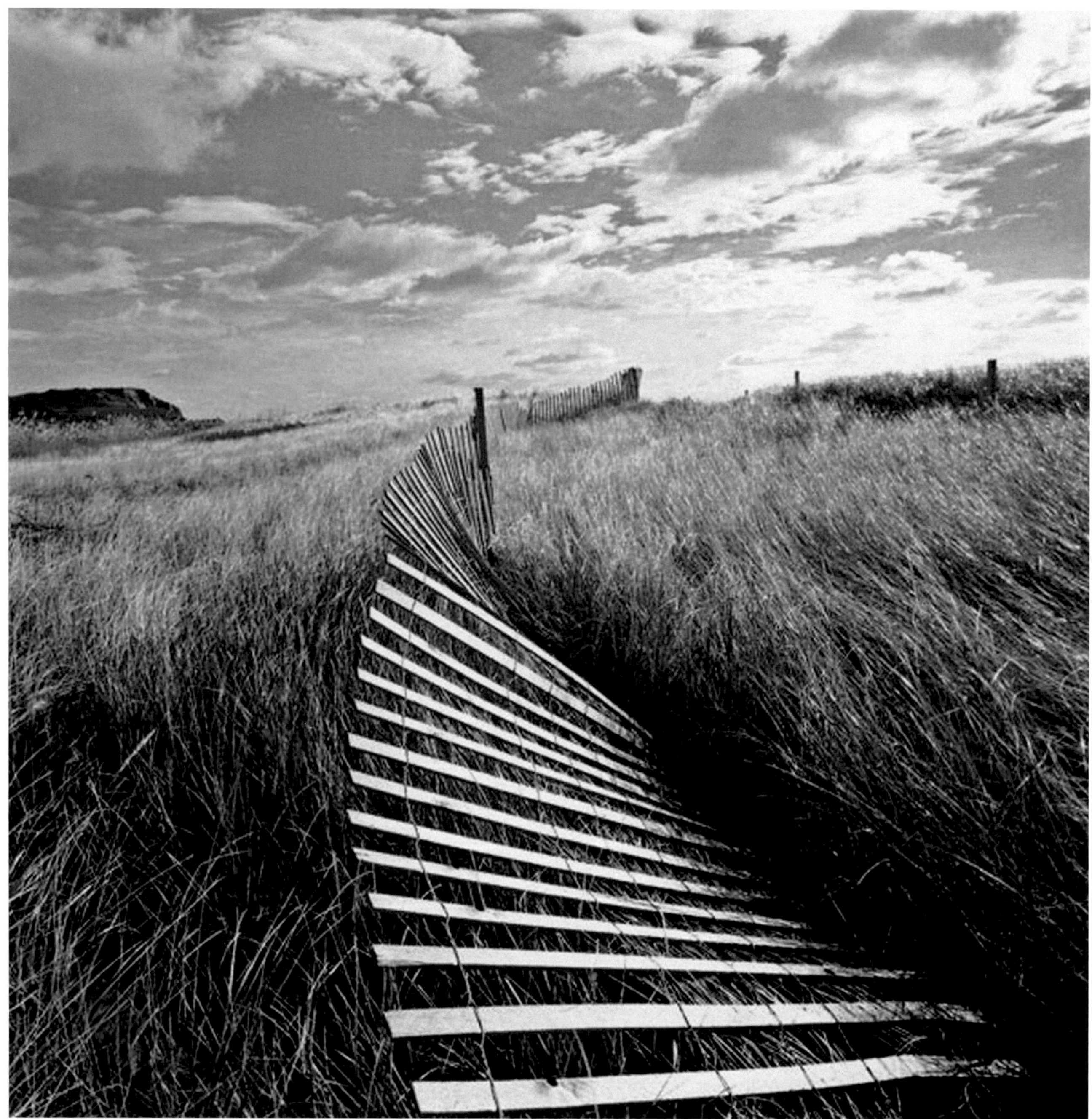

Lucy Vincent, 2003

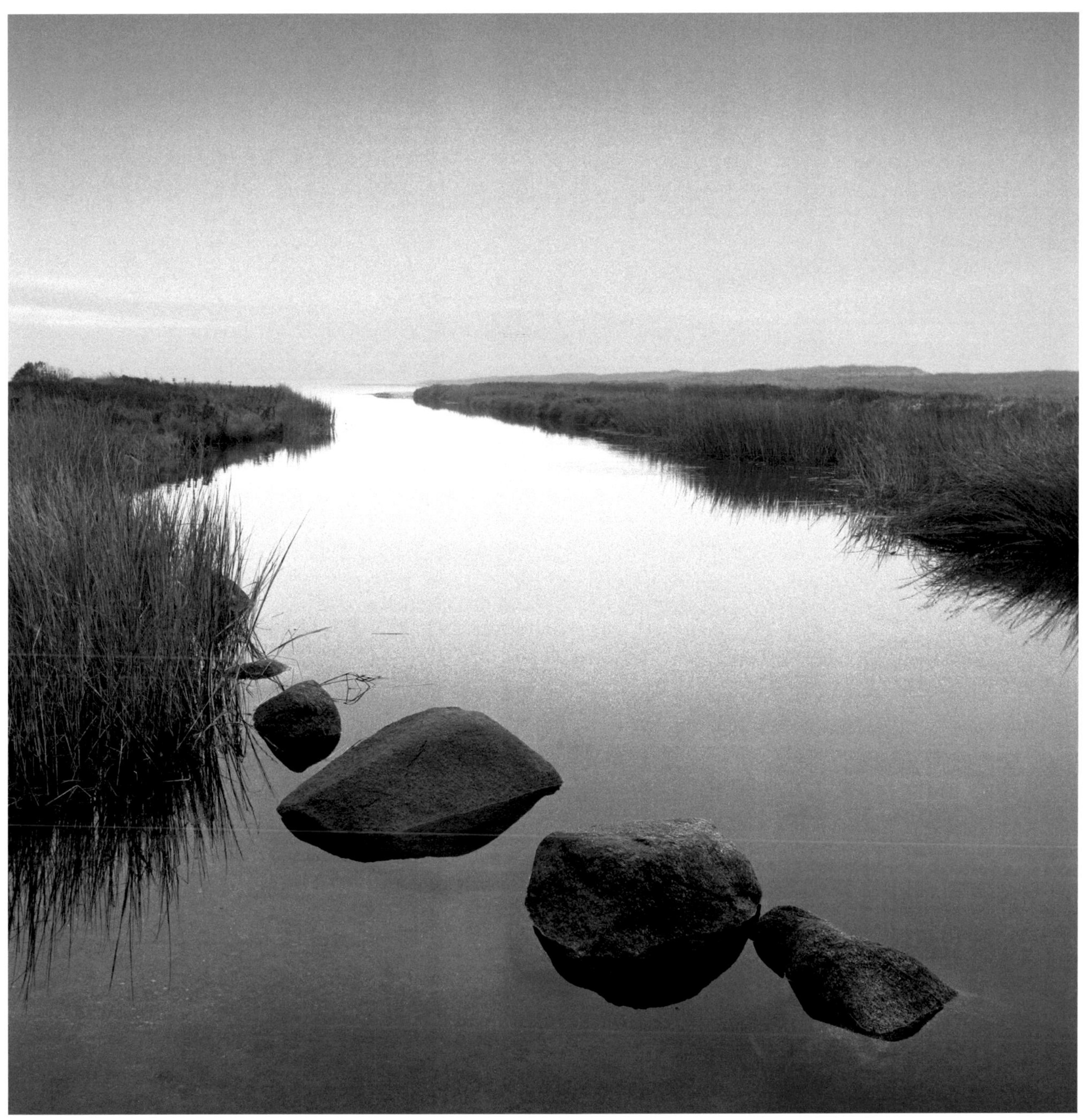

Tisbury Great Pond, 1999

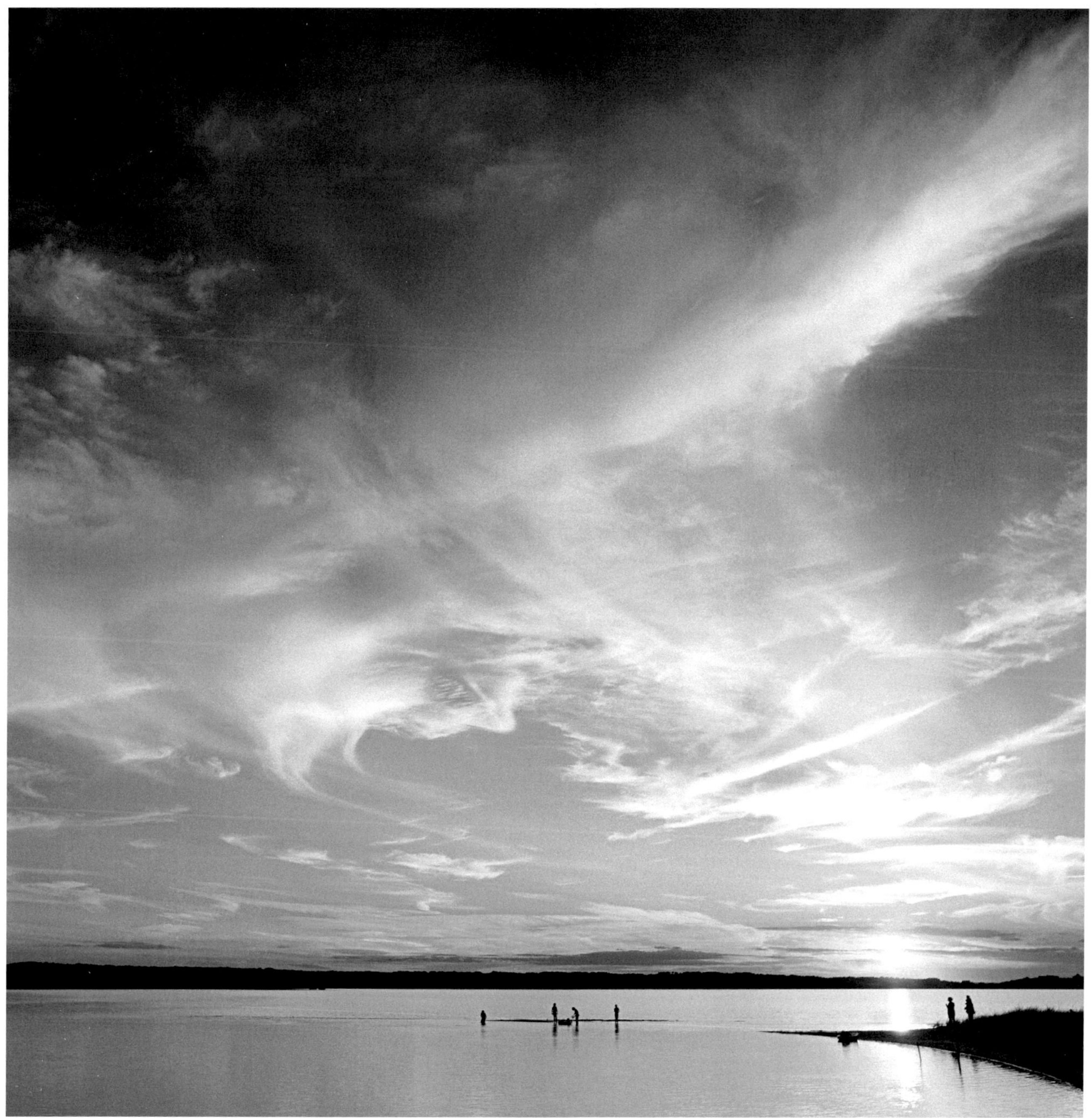

Toms Neck Point, 2001

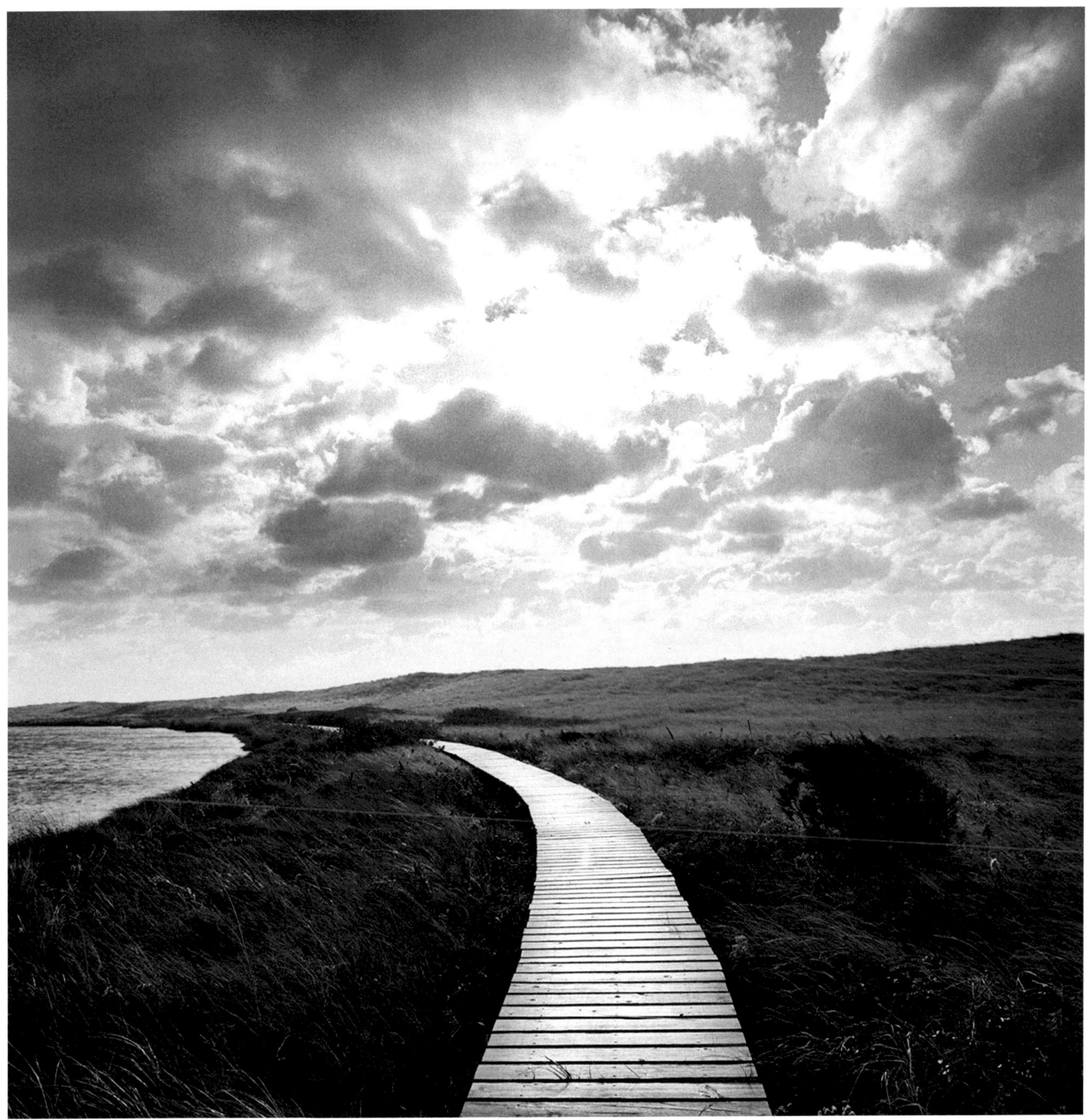

Long Point Preserve, 2006

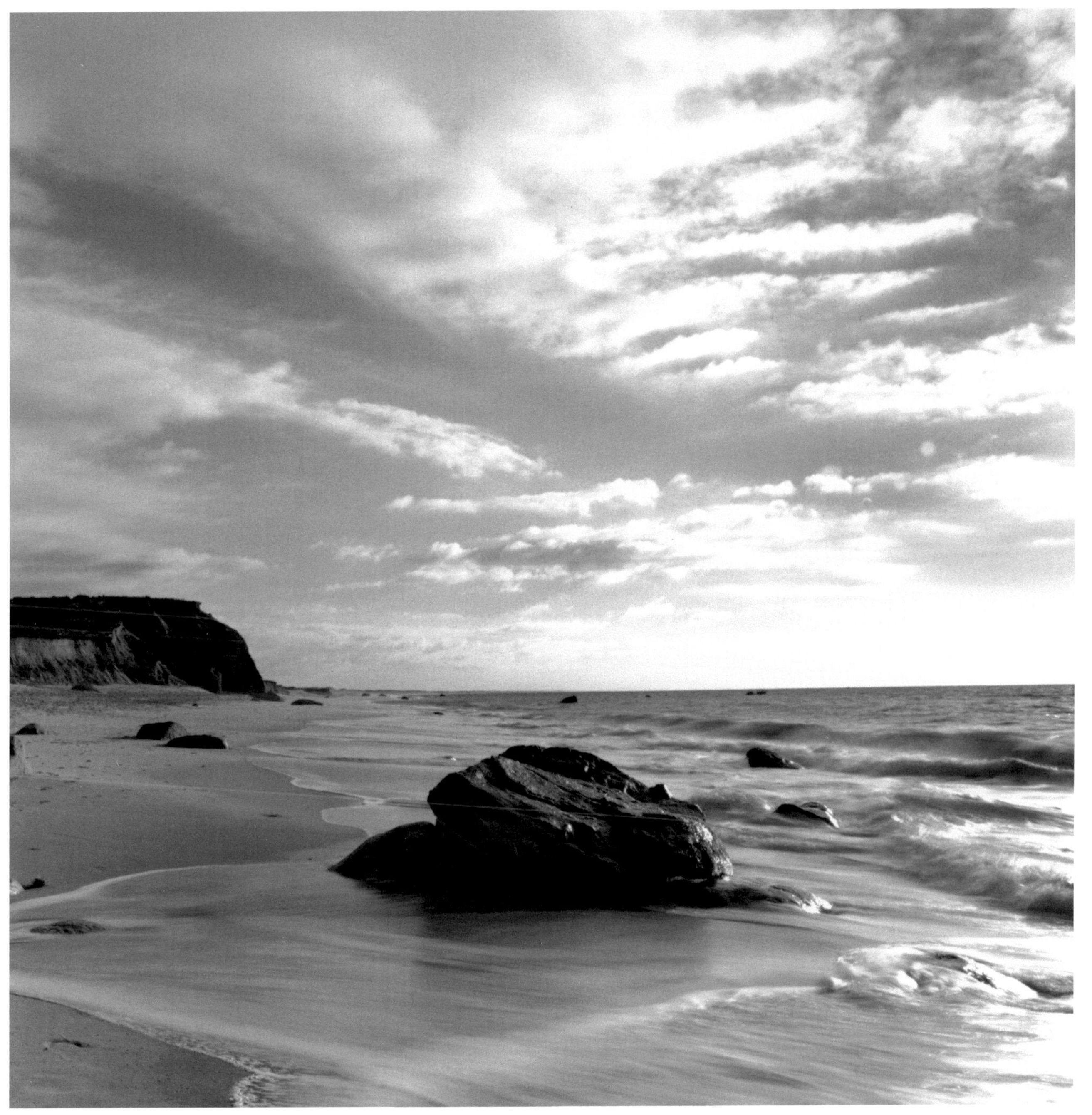
Wequobsque Cliffs, 1999

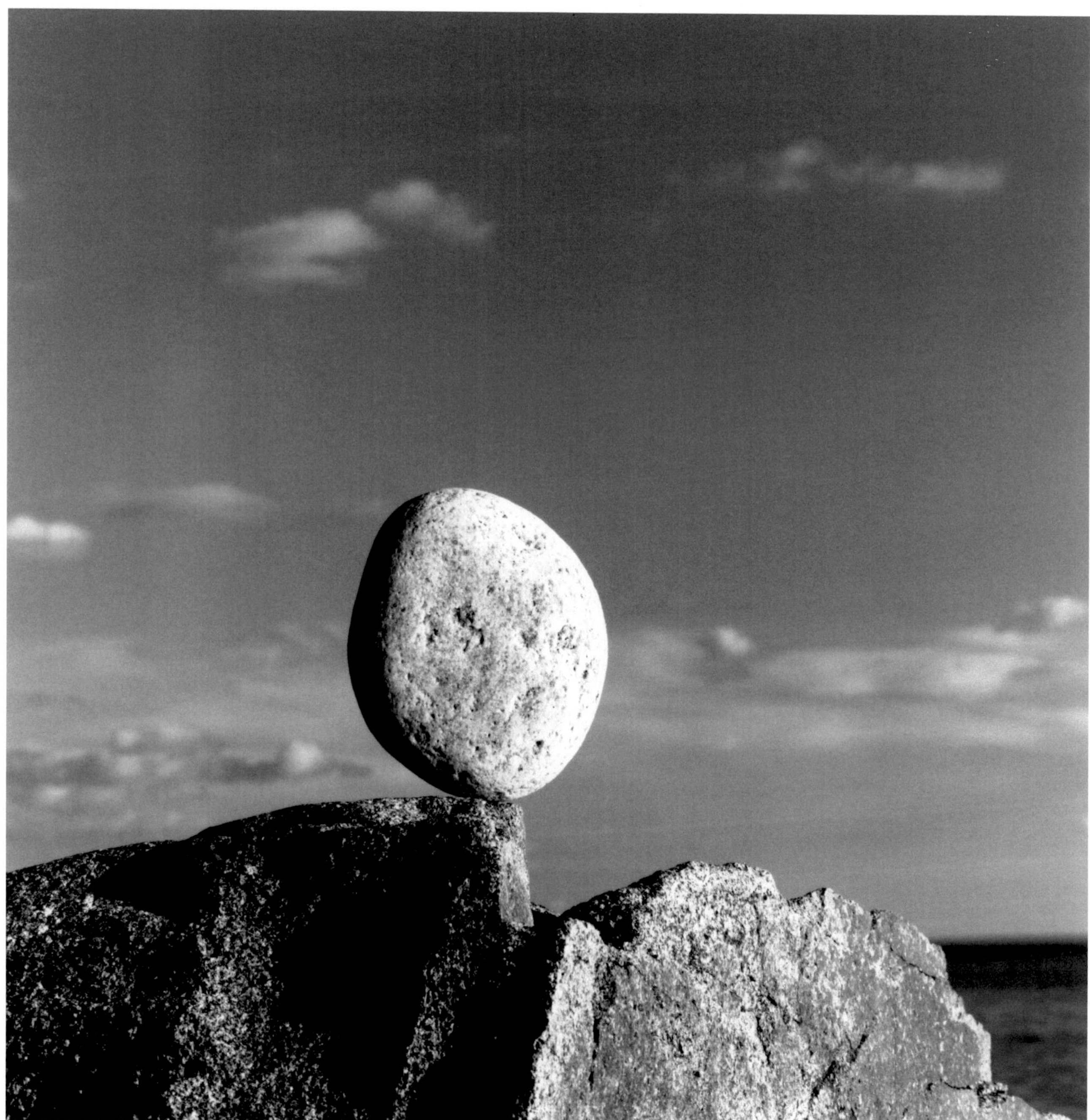

Aquinnah, 1999

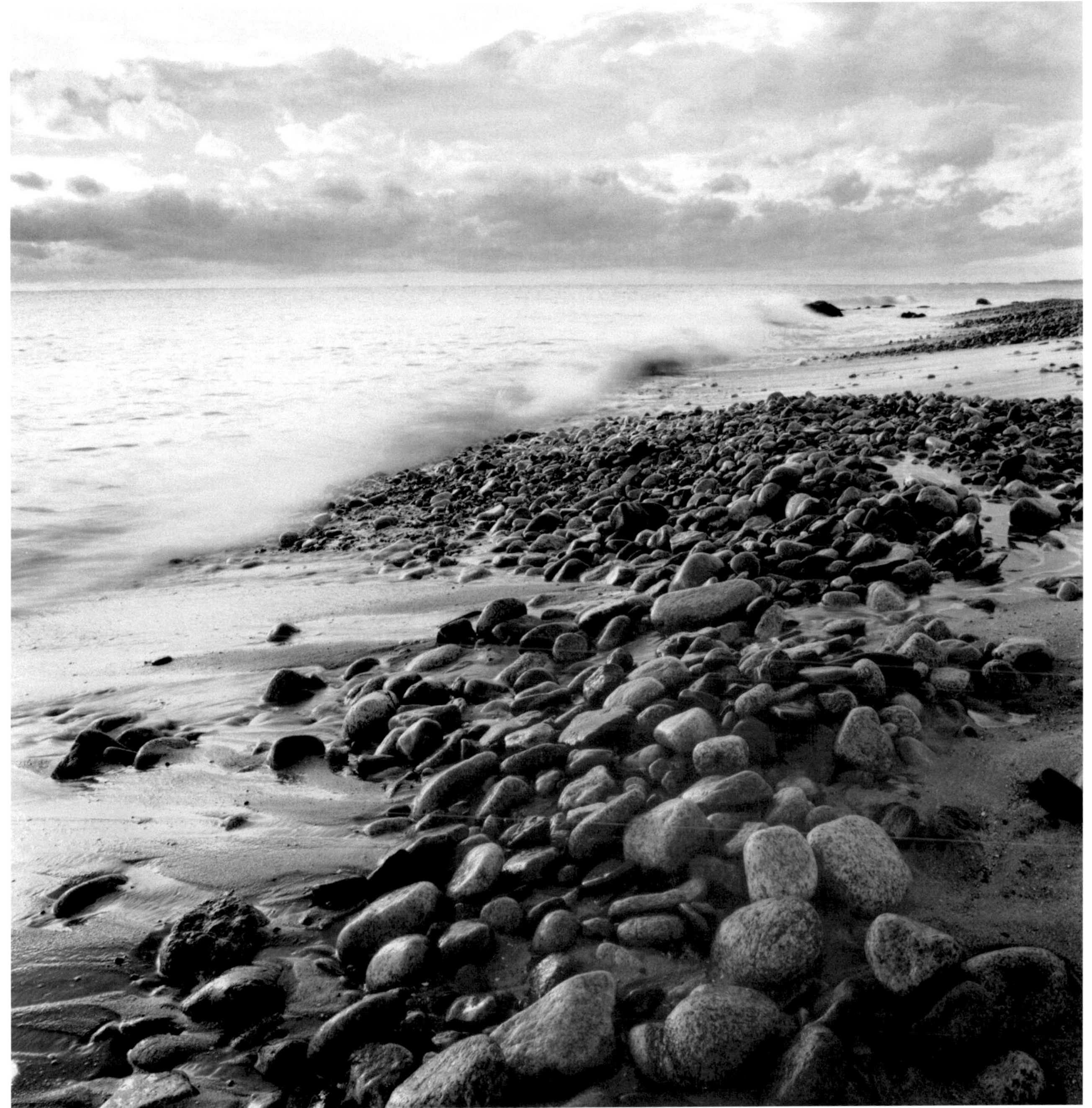

Aquinnah Beach, 1999

WHERE I AM GOING

RAINER MARIA RILKE

Again the murmur of my own deep life grows stronger,
flowing along wider shores.
Things grow ever more related to me,
and I see farther into their forms.
I become more trustful of the nameless.
My mind, like a bird,
rises from the oak tree into the wind,
and my heart sinks through the pond's reflected day
to where the fishes move.

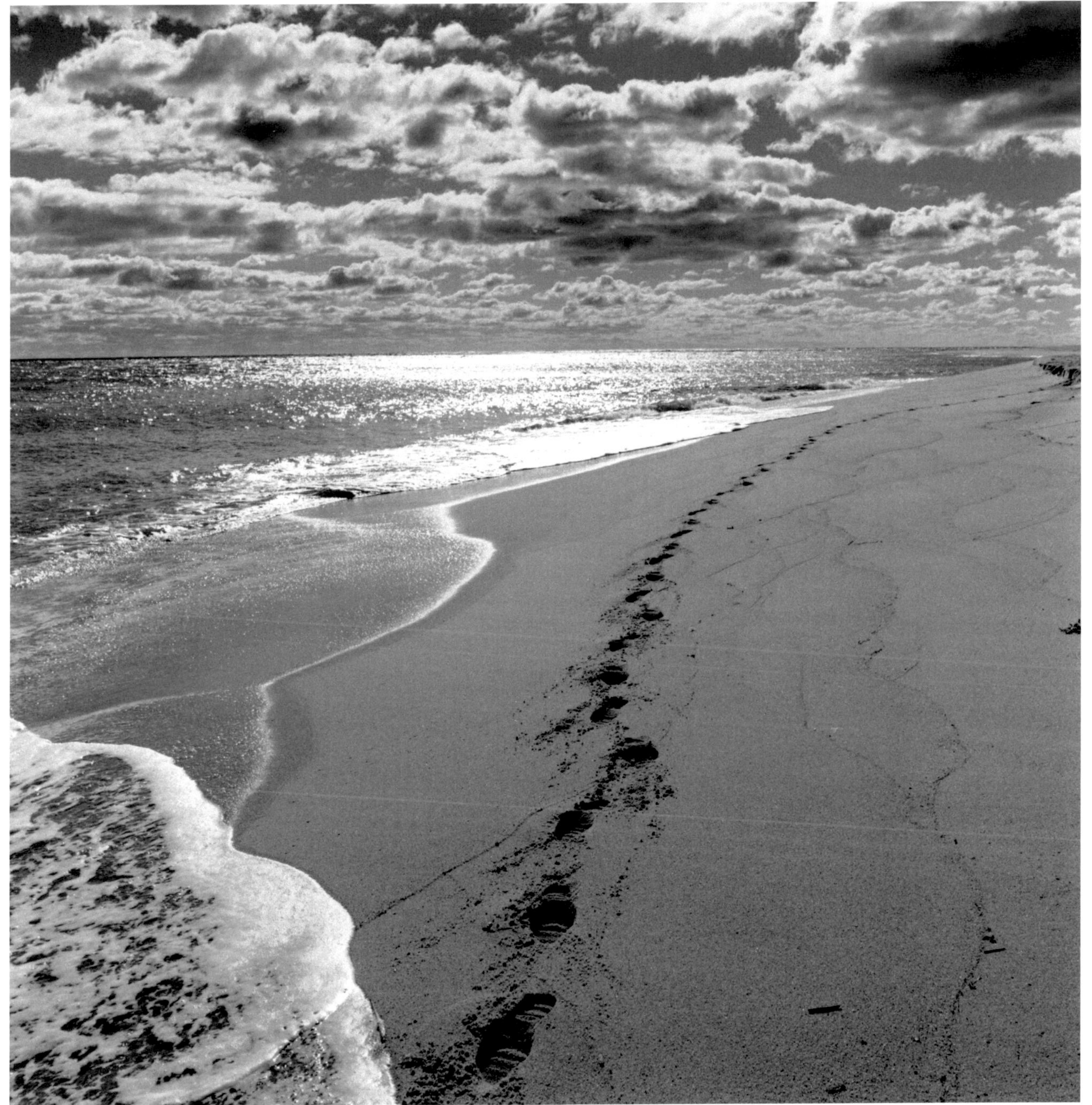

Katama Beach, 2006

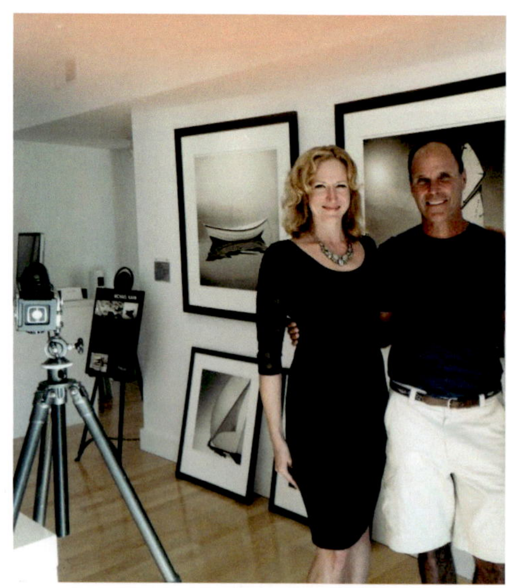

ABOUT THE AUTHOR

Internationally renowned photographer Michael Kahn's seascape and sailing photographs are exhibited in art galleries and museums throughout the world. Captured on a 1950s camera, the images are hand-produced as silver gelatin prints and finished to museum standards. For more information, please visit www.michaelkahn.com.

Christine Yurick is a poet and the founding editor of *Think Journal*. Along with being Michael's wife, she is the studio manager at Michael Kahn Photography. She enjoys pairing photographs with words and sharing their combined beauty with others.